Cultures and Cont

Barry Chazan • Robert Chazan • Benjamin M. Jacobs

Cultures and Contexts of Jewish Education

palgrave
macmillan

Barry Chazan
Hebrew University of Jerusalem
Spertus Institute for Jewish Learning
and Leadership
Chicago, Illinois, USA

Robert Chazan
New York University
New York, New York, USA

Benjamin M. Jacobs
The George Washington University
Washington, District of Columbia, USA

ISBN 978-3-319-84691-0   ISBN 978-3-319-51586-1   (eBook)
DOI 10.1007/978-3-319-51586-1

Cover illustration: Agata Gładykowska / Alamy Stock Photo

Printed on acid-free paper

This Palgrave Macmillan imprint is published by Springer Nature
The registered company is Springer International Publishing AG
The registered company address is: Gewerbestrasse 11, 6330 Cham, Switzerland

To Marissa and Ari Jacobs
And to the Chazan children and grandchildren

Acknowledgments

Each of us has spent a lifetime immersed in the world of Jewish education and Jewish civilization. Our first and most powerful teachers were in our homes (two of us in the same home), and our later educators included passionate classroom instructors, energetic camp counselors, inspired university professors, and bright and curious students, along with Jewish texts, scholarship, books, films, music, television, radio, magazines, websites, historical places, holy sites, museums, synagogues, organizations, institutions, workplaces, colleagues, mentors, friends, social groups, neighbors, and, to come full circle, our own families. The perspectives we share in this book were shaped by all these influences.

This volume also emerged out of many years of collaboration and close relationships among the authors. The original impetus for this project was the impulse of two siblings—senior scholars in their respective fields of education and Jewish studies—to work together for the first time on a book that would somehow meld their shared backgrounds and mutual interests while also reflecting their differing approaches to matters regarding Jewish life and learning. The inclusion of the third author soon thereafter was both strategic and instinctive, as the three colleagues had once constituted the faculty of the doctoral program in Education and Jewish Studies at New York University (in its early years, we sometimes had more instructors than students in the seminar we co-led, which of course made all of us students of each other). The dialogues that generated the ideas and claims we have advanced in this book began long before then and have continued ever since.

We are grateful to our partners on this project who helped bring it to fruition: Susan P. Fendrick, whose careful copyediting and insightful critiques of earlier drafts significantly enhanced our work; Sarah Nathan, who cleaned up our footnotes; Lisa Rivero, who compiled our index; and Erika Vogel, who adroitly managed the production of this book from start to finish. Thanks as well to the editorial and publishing staff at Palgrave Macmillan. Finally, our sincerest appreciation to the Memorial Foundation for Jewish Culture for a grant that supported our efforts. In the end, the views expressed and the choices made in this book are of course the responsibility of the authors alone.

CONTENTS

1 Pre-Modern Jewish Education   1
Biblical Israel and Its Educational Vision   2
The Mosaic Message   4
The Prophets and Their Educational Role   7
The Rabbis and Their Educational Leadership   10
The Educational Efforts and Achievements of the Rabbis   14
Maintaining Consistency Under Evolving Circumstances   18
The Jewish Transition into Western Christendom   23
The Jewish Worldview Maintained   28
Notes   29
Bibliography   30

2 The Crisis of Modernity   31
Redefining the Role of Religion in Western Societies   33
The New Egalitarian Society   35
Reconceptualizing Jewishness   39
Recreating Organizational Patterns in Western Societies   42
The Modern Challenges to Traditional Religion   45
Maintaining a Jewish Religious Worldview   48
*Adapting to the New: The Historic Achievements
of the Jewish People*   52
New Educational Perspectives and Cultures   55
Notes   56
Bibliography   58

3   America: Contexts and Cultures   59
  The Evolving Foundations of American Jewish Life   60
  Lessons from the Immigrant Experience   64
  Expansive Jewish Opportunities in America   65
  Organizing American Jewish Life   70
  The Holocaust in American Jewish Culture   71
  American Jews and Israel   73
  Secular American Jewish Culture   76
  Communal Cohesion and Its Difficulties   78
  Being Jewish in America   80
  Notes   81
  Bibliography   82

4   The Culture of American Jewish Schooling   83
  Education, Schooling, and the Culture of Schooling   85
  American Jewry's "Love Affair" with Public Schools   87
  The Creation of a Culture of American Jewish Schooling   92
  An Alternative Model for Jewish Schooling: The Day School   101
  Culture and Counterculture   106
  Notes   108
  Bibliography   112

5   The Counterculture of American Jewish Education   117
  The Making of a Jewish Educational Counterculture   121
  The "Next Gen" of the Jewish Education Counterculture   128
  Notes   135
  Bibliography   138

Epilogue   141
  In Search of a Paideia   141
  From Paideia *to Practice*   144
  Pedagogy   145
  Educators   145
  A Culture of Education   147
  Authority   147

Can It Happen? 148
Coda 150
Notes 150
Bibliography 151

Index 153

ABOUT THE AUTHORS

Barry Chazan is Professor Emeritus of the Hebrew University of Jerusalem and Professor of Education at the Spertus Institute for Jewish Learning and Leadership.

Robert Chazan is S.H. and Helen R. Scheuer Professor of Hebrew & Judaic Studies in the Skirball Department of Hebrew and Judaic Studies at New York University.

Benjamin M. Jacobs is a visiting associate professor in the Experiential Education & Jewish Cultural Arts program at The George Washington University.

PROLOGUE

In the religious polemics of medieval and early modern life, Jews often contrasted the literacy and learning in their own community with what they perceived to be the decidedly inferior educational accomplishments of their non-Jewish neighbors. While Jews knew that they constituted a small minority demographically, politically, and militarily, they were convinced nonetheless that they were unmatched in the realms of the spirit, knowledge, and ideas. Some modern Jews and their observers have asserted that the traditional Jewish emphasis on learning lies at the core of the remarkable scientific and literary achievements of modern Jews: for example, the stunning number of Jewish Nobel laureates in the widest possible range of intellectual endeavors. On every level and in every way, Jews over the ages customarily have taken great pride in Jewish educational achievement.

As modern Jews have confronted a new set of issues in radically altered circumstances, the sense of education as a critical element in Jewish life has been both reinforced and challenged. The importance of education has been proclaimed prominently in modern Jewish life, and Jews over the past few centuries have talked considerably about investment in Jewish education. At the same time, Jews have been widely attracted to and engaged in ideas, contents, and texts of other cultures in modernity.

Nowhere has the interaction of the age-old tradition of Jewish education with modern society been more apparent than in the contemporary American Jewish community. This community emerged suddenly and unexpectedly during the twentieth century as the world's largest and most powerful Jewry. A negligible element on the world Jewish scene until the late nineteenth century, the American Jewish community grew by leaps and bounds as a result of the massive migration from Eastern Europe that began during the 1880s. While for some people in the "old country," America was perceived as a land of license and licentiousness, for most eastern European immigrants—Jewish and non-Jewish alike—America was regarded as a land of equality and opportunity. Individual integration into the radically new American setting was complicated, but most Jewish immigrants—joining the prior and smaller set of American Jews— succeeded rather quickly in making a place for themselves in the land of equality and opportunity, and in fashioning a potent new force in world Jewry. The role of this new Jewish community was augmented markedly and painfully by the tragedy of the Holocaust, which destroyed the older centers of Jewish life and power, thus thrusting American Jewry more prominently into a central role in world Jewish life.

The dynamic of a mostly immigrant population with a long and rich educational tradition confronted by a dramatically new society, worldview, and emergent public schooling structure constitutes a fascinating chapter in Jewish life. It is the story of the interaction of two significantly different educational *paideia* and social visions. This interaction is the subject of our book.

Students of American Jewish education have not sufficiently appreciated the chasm that separates the modern and contemporary Jewish world from the environments that supported and challenged pre-modern Jewry. The differences between pre-modern and modern Jewish life are enormous, and their implications for American Jewish education are profound. Only when these differences are carefully clarified can the challenges and opportunities of contemporary American Jewish education be fully grasped. This book comes to clarify essential features of pre-modern Jewish education, describe the disruptions and achievements occasioned by the interaction with modernity and American culture, and reflect on the potential of contemporary American Jewish education in a twenty-first-century world.

* * *

In the pre-modern Jewish world, Jews by and large lived segregated from majority society, whether it was predominantly Islamic or predominantly Christian. This segregation was imposed by the non-Jewish majority for its purposes but was generally welcomed by the Jewish minority. Separation from the majority was by no means total; for example, economic needs required extensive majority-minority contact. Education, however, was rigorously segregated. All Jewish educational activities—in schools and outside of schools, for young and old alike—were organized, funded, and directed by the Jewish community.

This core reality of pre-modern Jewish life was radically altered as a result of the restructuring of Western states that began toward the end of the eighteenth century. In the new states created in the wake of the American and French revolutions, semi-autonomous communities and other bodies were stripped of their powers. One such body was the Jewish community, which had long had its own independent administrative structure, court system, social welfare agencies, and schools. In the modern nation-state, Jews enjoyed the new rights of citizenship and legal equality, while giving up many of the benefits associated with their essentially autonomous institutions—including, prominently, the Jewish educational system.

For pre-modern Jews, education was *ipso facto* Jewish education, but with the restructuring of modern Western states Jewish communal institutions were transformed from governmentally enforced and mandatory to entirely voluntary. In addition, Western states demanded of their newly enfranchised Jewish citizens that they become full participants in the new state culture, and secular education was key to this full participation. Those Jewish schools that did continue to operate had to alter their curricula to ensure that their students became full-blown French, English, or German citizens; in addition, considerable pressure was exerted to bring Jewish children into the emergent state schools.

Thus, for modern Jews, educational experiences (though not Jewish ones) have in the main been structured and often provided largely by the non-Jewish environment. With respect specifically to schooling of the young, standards have been dictated by the larger environment, and schooling has been provided primarily by the general educational system. The bulk of the modern Jewish schooling experience, then, has taken place in a non-Jewish context and is oriented in directions other than Jewish life and its enhancement. By definition, modern education is far more deeply influenced by the surrounding ambience than was the case in the pre-modern world. In sum, with integration into the modern nation-state has come a decisive change in the ways in which Jews of all ages are educated. This change and its implications have been of overwhelming significance to Jewish education in terms of its organization, authority, opportunities, and limitations.

The same set of changes has had major repercussions for the authority brought to bear on Jewish education. In the pre-modern world, where church and state were intimately linked, Jews did not have state authority of their own. Pre-modern Jews lived under the control of Islamic or

Christian rulers, who allowed Jews to administer their own internal affairs, including religion and education. In effect, this meant the backing of the non-Jewish political authorities for the religious hierarchy within the Jewish community. In medieval and early-modern western Christendom, for example, the ruling authorities ceded control of all aspects of Christian education to the Church and likewise control of all aspects of Jewish education to the rabbis. The rabbis exercised enormous power over Jewish life in general and the autonomous Jewish educational system in particular. The uniformity produced by this rabbinic control was impressive and in many ways served these Jewish communities well.

With modernity came the separation of church and state, which had a remarkable impact on Jewish life. Gone was the dominance of the religious elite in Jewish life in general and in Jewish religious and educational activities in particular. Jews were able to part ways with the former established religious authorities, and many enthusiastically did so. Alternative religious groupings emerged within the Jewish world, with each evolving version of Judaism developing its own set of educational views and commitments, and Jewish groupings not oriented toward religious identity made their appearance as well. Arguably the most powerful of these latter groupings were grounded in a vision of Jewish nationality and the drive to establish a nation-state that would express Jewish identity as it developed there. Here, too, the new vision of core Jewish identity carried with it an innovative set of Jewish educational goals and techniques.

The disintegration of the previously semi-autonomous and united Jewish community had enormous implications for the Jewish educational enterprise. Jewish education—heretofore dominated and controlled by the religious elite—now became Jewish educations (in the plural), a set of separate and independent educational undertakings, each guided by its own vision of the essential nature of Jewishness. No Jewish authorities were empowered any longer to declare illegitimate one or another of these visions or educational systems.

Traditional Jewish education had been steeped in the general authoritarianism of pre-modern life and thinking. A set of leaders within the Jewish fold was assumed to have mastered knowledge of Jewish tradition and thinking and was charged with the responsibility of transmitting their knowledge to the communities they led. While they used diverse methodologies—some quite text- and student-centered—their ultimate task and practice aimed at the transmission and inculcation of their understanding of Jewish tradition and its obligations. But with modernity came new understandings of societal organization and knowledge. No longer was any group within society (or any subgroup of society) venerated as the sole repository of wisdom—and indeed, the transmission of wisdom was no longer alone at the center of any educational vision. Modern Jewish education has had to consider the inclinations and predispositions of the learner and the needs imposed by his or her environment, along with the demands of the tradition being taught and the accumulated knowledge of the teacher.

Perhaps the most significant change flowing from modernity has involved changes in fundamental assumptions about the world in general and the Jewish world in particular. For pre-modern Jews, the basic mechanism of reality and history was control by the one and only God who had created the universe and continued to direct it. Historical developments were thought to result from fulfillment or non-fulfillment of the demands of the divine-human covenant. Jews perceived themselves as suffering in exile as punishment for the sins of their ancestors, with the sure faith that the same God who had exiled them would one day redeem them and lead them back to the land that had long been promised them.

Modernity changed these fundamental convictions for most Westerners, including most Jews. The deity was removed from the human scene in one of numerous ways; for example, the existence of God was denied outright; God was assumed to exist, but had long ago allowed the created world to function in accord with the laws (established by God) that govern it; God was understood as existing and affecting reality, but in ways that cannot be fathomed. Whatever the perspective adopted by individual Jews or Jewish movements, the result was to largely remove the workings of the divine-human covenant from an operative role in understanding historical processes.

Given this radical shift in the basic stance toward reality and history, Jews who have been attracted to the new views—and they have constituted the majority of modern Jewry—have had to construct innovative and naturalistically grounded (and widely varying) foundations for Jewish education. No longer perceived as a divine command, the imperative to Jewish education came to be rooted for many in the conviction that, over the ages, Jews have created a repository of wisdom that demands attention, admiration, and engagement. This wisdom resides both in core Jewish texts that must be carefully studied and in the history of the Jewish people as a dynamic and creative collective entity. Jewish education as a key to Jewish survival no longer revolves around fulfillment or non-fulfillment of the demands of the covenant, but study of the Jewish past provides invaluable insight into the successes and failures of diverse Jewish approaches to survival and human creativity.

While Jews can no longer claim the distinction of being the sole bearers of the divine-human covenant, careful study of the Jewish past alerts Jews to the many distinctive qualities of that past and confers a powerful sense of the dignity of Jewish identity. Precisely the lessons to be extracted from the Jewish legacy vary widely, focusing, for example, on Judaism's moral teachings, on its concern for all of humanity, on its commitment to maintaining the world's ecology, on the Hebrew language and the culture it has fostered, or on the centrality in Jewish history of the Land of Israel. No matter what the precise focus, the overall sense of modern educational approaches is the richness of the Jewish past and the need to grasp that richness and derive maximal benefit from it.

The obliteration of the semi-autonomous Jewish community, the demand that Jews integrate themselves into the Western states that granted them citizenship, and the redefining of Jewishness as either religious or ethnic/national identity constituted common developments all across the modern Western world. Nonetheless, salient differences between Westernized modern Jewish communities are identifiable and significant. Especially important for our purposes are the uniqueness of America and the special circumstances of the American Jewish community.

The European nation-states that emerged in the nineteenth century—pre-eminently France, England, and Germany—were heirs to millennia of national culture. Thus, the demands for Jewish absorption of and conformance to the national culture were intense. Jewish difference was legitimate only in the sphere of religion. Beyond the walls of the synagogue and the home, Jews were to comport themselves precisely like their non-Jewish neighbors.

In this respect, America was different. America could lay claim to nothing like the lengthy history of European national cultures; America was a newcomer on the nation-state scene. Moreover, Americans were deeply conscious of their society as grounded in immigration, and they largely embraced the immigrant experience and immigrants themselves. Thus, the pressures for conformity to a well-defined national culture in the United States were far weaker than in the European nation-states. As in the western sectors of Europe, Jews were defined fundamentally as a religious community, but there was space in America for a range of alternative Jewish cultural expressions as well.

In America, Jews could choose to identify themselves Jewishly in broader ways than in Europe. The American commitment to the division between church and state, as well as receptivity to diverse ethnic backgrounds and cultural histories, opened two portals—one religious, the other ethnic—for the shaping of new Jewish educational programs and institutions. Jewish education could be religious education, or it could be grounded in a cultural approach emphasizing the centrality of Jewish languages, Jewish cultures, and Jewish history. These dual portals enabled the creation of a much more diversified set of educational institutions and programs than was perceived as legitimate on the European scene. In our effort to understand American Jewish education, we have to be sensitive to the extent that American Jewry has enjoyed a special set of identity options and possible educational directions.

In the wake of World War II and subsequent technological, social, and political dynamics, world civilizations in general and American society in particular have undergone major changes. Globalization has enriched the economies and the social settings of most of the world and has been strongly felt in America. In addition, the technological revolution has been worldwide, with special impact in America. As a result, late twentieth- and early twenty-first-century Americans—Jews included—have become habituated to the stunning diversity of options available to them in all avenues of human life: economic opportunities, social mores, cultural standards, and identity typologies. The American openness to diversity, already felt by America's Jews prior to World War II, has become yet more prominent. The availability of multiple options for identifying Jewishly, which we have already cited as a unique feature of American Jewish life, has very much intensified in recent decades, and the tendency shows no sign of abating. This too has major implications for our understanding of American Jewish education.

* * *

Contemporary American Jewish education is deeply affected by the legacies bequeathed by the pre-modern period, by the revolution of modernity, and by the opportunities for diversity uniquely offered by America. Chapters 1 and 2 of this book focus on pre-modern and modern worldviews that were to affect the ideals and structures of American Jewish education. Chapter 3 focuses on the contexts and culture of twentieth-century America, as well as on expressions of Jewishness in the general culture of American film, literature, media, and public knowledge, all of which constitute educational means. Chapters 4 and 5 focus in a detailed fashion on the emergent culture and counterculture of Jewish education—formal (schooling) and informal (multiple venues)—that was to emerge in twentieth-century America in response to the particulars of American modernity. In the Epilogue, we reflect on opportunities that we believe this book raises for twenty-first-century American Jewish education.

We have titled this book *Cultures and Contexts of Jewish Education* in recognition of the fact that the enterprise of Jewish education, like the Jewish community that supports it, is hardly monolithic in character. Jews have moved extensively over the ages, locating themselves in a variety of cultures and in the process being deeply influenced by those cultures. Especially noteworthy is the radical disruption introduced by the process of modernization, which began in some places as early as the seventeenth century but came to fruition during the late eighteenth and nineteenth centuries. Against the backdrop of the reorganization of Western states and the obliteration of the semi-autonomous and powerful Jewish community, modern Western Jewries have included a wide range of internal Jewish worldviews, ranging from utter fidelity to pre-modern Jewish thinking to radical rejection of that thinking. While we are keenly aware of this diversity, we shall focus on those sectors of the modern Jewish community—especially of the American Jewish community—most engaged with modernity and its challenges.

Our title also alludes to educational theorist Jerome Bruner's *The Culture of Education* (1996), an assortment of essays on culture, context, and cognition. For Bruner, education is a powerful cultural device that reflects social and political circumstances and also shapes social mores and an individual's sense of self. Indeed, Bruner argues, culture is the very essence of what makes people human; what is more, education is the foremost guardian of culture and society. "The evolution of the hominid mind is linked to the development of a way of life where 'reality' is represented by a symbolism shared by members of a cultural community in which a technical-social way of life is both organized and construed in terms of that symbolism," Bruner writes. "This symbolic mode is not only shared by a community, but conserved, elaborated, and passed on to succeeding generations who, by virtue of this transmission, continue to maintain the culture's identity and way of life."[1]

Importantly, says Bruner, the conservation, elaboration, and transmission of culture—through the process of education—does not necessarily happen only in schools, though that is certainly one important venue for educational activity. Rather, the process of education encompasses a much broader complex of experience, learning, and growth. As Bruner puts it, "Education does not only occur in classrooms, but around the dinner table when family members try to make joint sense of what happened that day, or when kids try to help each other make sense of the adult world, or when a master and apprentice interact on the job."[2]

Educational historian Lawrence Cremin also depicted education as occurring in many more venues than just schools and classrooms:

> Every family has a curriculum, which it teaches quite deliberately and systematically over time. Every church and synagogue has a curriculum, which it teaches deliberately and systematically over time—the Old and New Testaments, after all, are among our oldest curricula... And every employer has a curriculum, which he teaches deliberately and systematically over time; and the curriculum includes not only the technical skills ... but also the social skills of carrying out those activities in concert with others... One can go on to point out that libraries have curricula, museums have curricula, boy scout troops have curricula, and day-care centers have curricula, and most important, perhaps, radio and television stations have curricula—and by these curricula I refer not only to programs labeled educational but also to news broadcasts and documentaries (which presumably inform), to commercials (which teach people to want), and to soap operas (which reinforce common myths and values).[3]

In Cremin's view, education is comprehensive, occurring regularly in all facets of society and in the midst of day-to-day life; it is relational, occurring regularly in all interactions between individuals; and it is public, occurring regularly in the service of communal values and with implications for public life. In these ways, education is society's cultural linchpin, or as Cremin referred to it, the nation's *paideia*.

In this book, we take a similarly expansive view of education and describe the way education evolved as a central facet of Jewish life, as well as the various cultures of education manifested in the Jewish community over time. Our focus is not on the history of Jewish educational formats and structures—though those feature prominently in the latter chapters of the book—but rather on the ideational, intellectual, and cultural motifs of pre-modern, early modern, and modern Jewry, and their impact on the shaping of modern American Jewish education. We explore the concept of Jewish *paideia* in the remote Jewish past, its loss in modernity, and the need for a new *paideia* for American Jewish life today.

Our work combines historical background and insight with educational expertise on both the theoretical and practical level. Each of the three authors brings one of these disciplinary tools to the task. One is a historian of the Jews, who has written extensively on the contours of Jewish society, including the history of Jewish education; a second is a philosopher of education, who has written widely on Jewish educational visions and objectives; the third is a curriculum scholar and educational historian, deeply concerned with the diverse cultures and practices of modern Jewish education. Essential to the success of this undertaking is an integration of our three domains.

NOTES

1. Jerome Bruner, *The Culture of Education* (Cambridge, MA: Harvard University Press, 1996), 3.
2. Ibid., xi.
3. Lawrence A. Cremin, *Public Education* (New York: Basic Books, 1976), 22.

BIBLIOGRAPHY

Bruner, Jerome. 1996. *The Culture of Education*. Cambridge, MA: Harvard University Press.
Cremin, Lawrence A. 1976. *Public Education*. New York: Basic Books.

CHAPTER 1

Pre-Modern Jewish Education

The human quest for knowledge takes many forms. Most basic of all, individuals and groups attempt to understand aspects of their immediate surroundings by observing and comprehending, for example, the flora and fauna with which they live. These rudimentary efforts involve no ulterior motives and no intrinsic desire for control or gain. Rather, the motivation is pure and joyous—the desire to know for its own sake. Humans seek knowledge for utilitarian purposes as well, including scientific advancement, technological control of the environment, economic improvement and exploitation, and backing for political or religious power. Beyond these kinds of understanding—whether for its own sake or for utilitarian purposes—the pursuit of knowledge sometimes involves the simplest and yet profoundest quest: to understand oneself and one's universe and to translate that understanding into constructive and meaningful living. How did the universe start? Where did I come from? Who am I? What is my purpose in life? What course of life is best?

The Tanakh (the three-part Hebrew Bible) is not mainly concerned with knowledge for its own sake or for the purpose of control. Its essential project is to connect human existence to divine providence: What is the overall nature of the universe God created? How does human history unfold because of or despite God's control? What can humans do in the face of radical uncertainty? How can humans structure their lives in such a way as to make them acceptable to the God who created and controls the cosmos?

© The Author(s) 2017
B. Chazan et al., *Cultures and Contexts of Jewish Education*,
DOI 10.1007/978-3-319-51586-1_1

While these momentous questions invite a wide range of potential responses, the educational aim of the Tanakh is in fact quite focused. From the very beginning of the Hebrew Bible, the dynamics of human history are clearly delineated, with implications for the ways in which individual Jews and Jewish communities as a whole should structure their actions. Those lessons that are not conveyed through historic events (e.g., the patriarchal stories, the Israelite wanderings in the wilderness, or Israelite history in Canaan) are delivered through law codes (e.g., much of Leviticus) or didactically by visionary leaders (e.g., Moses, the prophets). Knowing how the universe and history work shapes the patterns of behavior toward which individuals and the community must strive.

The Tanakh is not merely a story of Israelite origins, nor is it simply a repository of divine commandments. It is rather, above all, a guidebook for human behavior grounded in faith in God and the conviction of divine control of history. Pre-modern Jewish education was solidly anchored in this biblical sense of God and history and its implications. The Tanakh is the core text of Jewish life, and it thus sets the fundamental agenda for the Jewish educational enterprise over the ages.[1]

BIBLICAL ISRAEL AND ITS EDUCATIONAL VISION

In the biblical view, human fate derives from success or failure in meeting the demands of the one and only God, who created and sustains the universe. To the extent that divine demands are met, humans will enjoy blessing; to the extent that they are not met, the result will be tribulation and suffering. The very first two humans, Adam and Eve, are given but one command— to refrain from eating the fruit of the Tree of Knowledge. Their failure to observe this injunction triggers expulsion from Eden and travail for all of subsequent humanity. It is a painful lesson to learn, but the message is clear: Human wellbeing derives from fulfilling God's commandments. Failure to do so eventuates in divinely inflicted punishment and attendant human suffering.

As the Bible pursues its account of early humanity, this message is regularly reinforced. Although the specific shortcomings of Noah's peers are not identified, their wide-ranging sinfulness leads to massive punishment, in effect the eradication of almost all of humanity. To be sure, a positive note is struck here as well: Noah, who fulfilled the divine demands imposed upon human behavior, survives the destruction and forms the kernel of a revived humanity. Misbehavior entails punishment and suffering; proper behavior wins God's favor and results in blessing.

With the appearance of Abraham, a vital new element is added to the biblical narrative: the selection of one human family/community as God's unique partners. Why God should have decided to do so is not clear, and the reasons for selecting Abraham as God's human partner are not at all obvious. The implications of this momentous change and choice, however, are both clear and obvious. God henceforth makes specific demands on the chosen covenantal community. Thus, in addition to the fulfillment or flouting of generalized human norms, the fate of God's human partners will be determined by their successes or failures in meeting the special demands of their covenant with God.

While the biblical stories of early humanity focused on humans' failure to meet divine requirements and resultant punishment, the Abraham saga revolves around his and his family's unique success in fulfilling special and painful divine expectations. After the touching account of the birth of a longed-for son to the aged Abraham and Sarah, God appears with the following peremptory order:

> Take your son, your one and only son Isaac, whom you love, and go to the land of Moriah. There you shall offer him as a sacrifice on one of the heights that I shall show you.[2]

This divine demand is harrowing. Yet Abraham, who had argued vigorously with God in opposition to the divine decision to destroy Sodom and Gomorrah, acquiesces silently, setting out immediately to do God's will.

The sacrifice of his son is ultimately aborted, but God recognizes in extraordinary fashion Abraham's readiness to fulfill this painful order.

> Then the angel of the Lord called from heaven a second time to Abraham and said: "This is the word of the Lord: By my own self I swear that, because you have done this and have not withheld your son, your only son, I shall bless you abundantly and make your descendants as numerous as the stars in the sky or the grains of sand on the seashore. Your descendants will possess the cities of their enemies. All nations on earth will wish to be blessed as your descendants are blessed, because you have been obedient to me."[3]

All human beings live under the watchful eye of the one and only God and are judged in accord with how well or how poorly they fulfill God's fundamental rules. The chosen community in addition bears the burden and enjoys the blessing of living under an additional set of obligations, which they must understand and fulfill.

It is easy to dismiss these early biblical incidents as simple folklore, and modern biblical scholars have traced many of these stories back to the storehouse of ancient Near Eastern mythology. Such dismissal, however, is misguided. While the stories may be folkloristic in style and may even be borrowed, they are reworked to provide an authentic—indeed a fundamental—Israelite and subsequently Jewish message: There is only one God in the world; that God created heaven and earth and controls the destiny of the universe and its human inhabitants; the core dynamic of human fate involves satisfying or affronting the one and only God. This crucial message is firmly established at the outset of the biblical narrative; it then sets the stage for further developments, as the Israelites emerge onto the stage of history as God's chosen partners. It had enormous implications for all of pre-modern Jewish life and became the fundamental tenet of pre-modern Jewish education.

The Mosaic Message

With Moses and the exodus from Egypt, the demands laid upon God's partner community take on new specificity. The biblical narrative moves in five books from the creation of the world down through the preparations to enter the Holy Land, a period of thousands of years according to the biblical reckoning. Yet the overwhelming bulk of this narrative is devoted to the 40 years of the exodus from Egypt and wilderness wandering. The majority of this account involves specification of a very wide range of divine obligations laid upon the Israelites.

Moses repeatedly emphasizes the results of success or failure in fulfillment of the commandments he communicates. Deuteronomy, the last of the five books of the Torah, consists largely of lengthy addresses by Moses. As he prepares to take leave of his people and they make ready to enter the land promised to them, Moses undertakes one final effort to convey to them the core dynamic of Israelite history. In his closing messages, Moses emphasizes one last time the covenant between God and Israel, the rewards for fulfillment of the demands of this covenant, and the punishments for its neglect. The dramatic finality of these closing addresses makes them critically important to traditional Jewish thinking over the ages and thus to the fundamental patterns of traditional Jewish education.

In his final exhortation, Moses highlights the punishments attendant upon neglect of the covenant, beginning with God mustering the forces of nature against sinful Israel:

> The Lord will let loose against you calamity, panic, and frustration in all the enterprises you undertake, so that you shall soon be utterly wiped out because of your evildoing in forsaking me. The Lord will make pestilence cling to you, until he has put an end to you in the land that you are entering to possess. The Lord will strike you with consumption, fever, and inflammation, with scorching heat and drought, with blight and mildew; they shall hound you until you perish. The skies above your head shall be copper and the earth under you iron. The Lord will make the rain of your land dust, and sand shall drop on you from the sky, until you perish.[4]

While these calamities might otherwise be perceived simply as natural misfortunes, Moses paints a picture in which these natural disasters—should they take place—must be understood as divine punishment, occasioned by Israel's forsaking its covenant with God.

The same must also be understood with respect to invasion by enemy forces and the violence they inflict:

> The Lord will put you to rout before your enemies; you shall march out against them by a single road, but flee from them by many roads; and you shall become a horror to all the kingdoms of the earth. Your carcasses shall become food for all the birds of the sky and all the beasts of the earth, with none to frighten them off... Your sons and daughters shall be delivered to another people, while you look on; and your eyes shall strain for them constantly, but you shall be helpless. A people you do not know shall eat up the produce of your soil and all your gains; you shall be abused and downtrodden continually, until you are driven mad by what your eyes behold.[5]

Israel's victories over inevitable foes in the land they are entering are by no means assured. Those victories must be earned, and can only be won through fulfillment of the divine covenant that Moses has spelled out in great detail.

The depictions of natural calamity and suffering at the hands of enemies in Canaan as a result of neglect of the covenant are horrific; there is, however, even worse in store for sinful Israel. Maintenance of their place in the land promised to them is by no means a given. Neglect of the covenant will ultimately lead to exile from the territory they are joyfully poised to enter. Moses concludes his catalogue of the suffering to be inflicted with the following:

The Lord will scatter you among all the peoples from one end of the earth to the other, and there you shall serve other gods, wood and stone, whom neither you nor your ancestors have experienced. Yet even among those nations you shall find no peace, nor shall your foot find a place to rest. The Lord will give you there an anguished heart and eyes that pine and a despondent spirit. The life you face shall be precarious; you shall be in terror night and day, with no assurance of survival. In the morning, you shall say "If only it were evening!" and in the evening you shall say "If only it were morning!"—because of what your heart will dread and your eyes will see. The Lord will send you back to Egypt in galleys, by a route I told you that you would not see again. There you shall offer yourselves for sale to your enemies as male and female slaves, but none will buy.[6]

This is the most frightening of the predictions with which Moses's closing address ends. All the benefits achieved under Moses's leadership will be undone. The land into which the Israelites are poised to enter will be lost—surely a drastic message for the people who had traveled for 40 years through the wilderness in anticipation of reaching the land promised to their ancestors. Moreover, the loss of the Promised Land will lead to the Israelites being scattered all across the known world. Life in this exile and dissemination among all peoples will be worse even than death, with profound psychological pain at every moment. Eventually, the exiled Israelites will make their way ignominiously back to Egypt, where they will be unable even to resume their positions as slaves, since no one will be willing to purchase them. All the blessings enjoyed under Mosaic leadership will be lost as a result of abandonment of the covenant.

To be sure, this painful message is not Moses's final word. The covenant will still remain in effect, Israel's failures and the attendant punishment of exile from the land and scattering among the nations notwithstanding. Genuine repentance will evoke divine mercy and resumption of the blessings of the covenant:

When all these things befall you—the blessing and the curse that I have set before you—and you take them to heart amidst the various nations to which the Lord your God has banished you, and you return to the Lord your God, and you and your children heed his command with all your heart and soul, just as I enjoin upon you this day, then the Lord your God will restore your fortunes and take you back in love. He will bring you together again from all the peoples where the Lord your God has scattered you. Even if your outcasts are at the ends of the world, from there the Lord your God will gather you. And the Lord your God will bring you to the land that your fathers possessed, and you shall possess it.[7]

Banishment and scattering constitute the nadir of Israel's fortunes, but even this ultimate punishment can be reversed through a genuine return to the covenant.

This biblical depiction of God, humanity, the Israelite nation, the covenant, and the historical process that governs the relationship among them is both embedded in and necessitates an educational process. Teaching is one of Moses' most important functions as leader of the Israelites; one of his central tasks—especially but certainly not exclusively toward the end of the Torah—is to convey the nature of the covenant, the specific demands of the covenant, and the results of fulfillment or non-fulfillment of these demands. The highly persuasive—indeed compelling—teaching Moses does in Deuteronomy is intended to have the effect of exhorting the people to action, not mere understanding. The intense and at times horrific nature of his final speech is meant to rouse in the Israelites an emotional response that compels them to follow the divine instructions. Moses was both a law transmitter and a law explicator for the Israelites. The chain of transmission of Jewish law that, according to the rabbis of the Mishnah, began with Moses at Sinai and continued down through the ages, was a succession not of the custodians of an abstract law code, but rather of the conveyers, interpreters, and teachers of Jewish obligations and responsibilities.

Significantly, Moses is identified in Jewish tradition as *Moshe Rabbeinu*, Our Rabbi Moses or Moses Our Teacher. This nomenclature highlights the extent to which Jews over the ages viewed Moses as their premier educator. By retroactively conferring on Moses the title of "rabbi/teacher," Jews were also in effect valorizing their own rabbinic leaders as successors to Moses and Israel's foremost educators. This simple act of naming reinforced the persistent centrality of education and rabbinic leadership in the life of the Jewish community.

THE PROPHETS AND THEIR EDUCATIONAL ROLE

The next six books of the Hebrew Bible—a historical narrative that moves from the entry into Canaan to the exile into Babylonia some six centuries later—are often referred to by modern biblical scholars as the "Deuteronomic History," since the scheme that dominates these books is contained in the Mosaic message delivered in Deuteronomy.[8] Repeatedly, Israelite suffering is projected as the result of failure to fulfill the demands of the covenant. As the Israelites battle their way into Canaan, they enjoy victories and suffer defeats, and the latter are regularly attributed to their failure to do God's will. Once settled in the land, the Israelites endure the normal human allotment of success and failure, but these shifts in fortune are by no means treated as normal. The successes are portrayed as result-ing from fulfillment of divine will, and the failures are ascribed to neglect of the covenant.

Into this narrative of Israelite fortunes in Canaan, an important new element is added. God seeks to remind the Israelites of their obliga-tions and of the price to be paid for neglect of these obligations. While God recognizes, as it were, the need for cultic and political stability in Israelite society and establishes a hereditary priesthood and a hereditary monarchy, God is also cognizant of the Israelite potential for neglect of the covenant and regularly dispatches messengers to remind his people of their covenant with him, the demands of that covenant, and the results of fulfillment or non-fulfillment of those demands. These messengers—the prophets—come from no special strand of Israelite society; they are indi-vidually selected and sent directly by God to their errant contemporaries. The task of the prophets is onerous: They are to bring a message of failure and its consequences to a people who do not wish to listen.

The prophets feature prominently in the six historical books that begin with Joshua and end with II Kings. In addition, the second section of the three-part Hebrew Bible includes a number of further books that are presented as the direct utterances of these divinely dispatched messengers. The two sets of depictions dovetail nicely. The Israelite shortcomings—obstinacy and intransigence—are the same, as is the core message that God will reward fulfillment of the covenant and will punish its neglect.

The setting in which the classical prophets delivered their message involved constantly evolving dangers within Canaan. In the eighth cen-tury, however, a new and far more menacing threat materialized from outside Canaan. The powerful Mesopotamian empire of the Assyrians began a process of expansion westward toward the Mediterranean. Local polities in the path of this expansion faced the difficult choice between capitulation to Assyrian rule and resistance. By this time, the Israelites had split into two monarchies, the Israelite kingdom of the north and the Judean kingdom of the south. It was against the threatening backdrop of the Assyrian invasion that the classical prophets initially delivered their message: a reprise (or in terms of date of composition, probably an early formulation) of the Mosaic warning, emphasizing that the Assyrian threat was not a simple political or military matter. In effect, God was threat-ening to bring punishment upon his recalcitrant people in the form of the Assyrians. The key to the Israelite and Judean future—once again, as always—lay in fulfillment of the covenant.

The Israelites and the Judeans chose alternative paths for meeting the Assyrian threat. The Israelites of the north opted to resist, fought the Assyrians, lost, and suffered the standard Assyrian punishment of death, exile, and dispersal, thus disappearing forever from history. For the Judean writers who composed the narrative that included the downfall of the northern kingdom, this constituted the ultimate example of the workings of divinely controlled history. The Israelites of the north had rejected their covenantal responsibilities and had suffered the ultimate consequence: total obliteration. The author(s) of II Kings explains the catastrophe at some length:

> This happened because the Israelites sinned against the Lord their God, who had freed them from the land of Egypt, from the hand of Pharaoh king of Egypt. They worshipped other gods and followed the customs of the nations the Lord had dispossessed before the Israelites and the customs the kings of Israel had practiced.[9]

The author(s) of II Kings notes explicitly the prophetic voices that portrayed the dangers attendant on Israelite sinfulness, warned of the punishments in the offing, and urged the Israelite people to repent and thus avert the harsh divine decree.

> The Lord warned Israel and Judah by every prophet [and] every seer, saying: "Turn back from your wicked ways, and observe my commandments and my laws, according to all the teaching that I commanded your fathers and that I transmitted through my servants the prophets..." But they did not obey; they stiffened their necks, like their fathers who did not have faith in the Lord their God; they spurned his laws and the covenant that he had made with their fathers and the warnings he had given them... The Lord was incensed at Israel, and he banished them from his presence. None was left but the tribe of Judah alone.[10]

The Assyrian onslaught and the mass deportation of the Israelites of the north are interpreted in II Kings as the result of the dismal failure to fulfill the responsibilities enjoined by the covenant.[11]

Eventually, the Judeans fell into disfavor with their imperial overlords, by this time the Babylonian successors to the Assyrians. In the late sixth century, the Judeans rebelled against Babylonia, and they too suffered exile, a technique adopted by the Babylonians from their Assyrian predecessors. The exile at the hands of the Babylonians was harsh: Jerusalem and its temple were destroyed, and the Judean population was deported from the Land of Israel. However, the damage inflicted was not as thorough as that suffered by the Israelite kingdom of the north. The Judeans in exile were allowed to congregate in groups and thus maintained their communal identity and faith. The Judeans survived their exile and were eventually permitted by the next imperial authorities, the Persians, to return to the Land of Israel, which some of them chose to do.

The message of the first section of the Hebrew Bible—the record of humanity and God's chosen people from creation through the return from Egyptian bondage and the desert wanderings—is maintained in the second section as well, in its account of the Israelites and Judeans from their entry into Canaan through the destruction of the northern kingdom and then on to exile of the Judeans at the hands of the Babylonians. History reflects the will of God, and the vicissitudes of history are activated by human behaviors, positive or negative. More specifically for Israel, changing fortunes reflect success or failure in fulfilling the special obligations laid upon it by God. In the biblical account, the people of Israel periodically suffered catastrophe as a result of its shortcomings.

Education in ancient Israel entailed, in sum, conveying knowledge of the covenant and encouraging its fulfillment, purposefully orienting the Israelites to their fate, and guiding the community toward a happier future. In this sense, Moses and the prophets served in effect as the divinely appointed educators of their people. Their educational message was clear and unambiguous. The key to the future of Israel as a community and to the wellbeing of individual Jews lay in recognition of God's role in the universe and human history and in full acceptance of this role. Israel's fate was dependent ultimately on fulfillment of the divinely ordained demands of the covenant.

The Rabbis and Their Educational Leadership

During the period of Persian domination of the ancient Near East (the late sixth through the late fourth pre-Christian centuries), the Judean diaspora that had been established in Mesopotamia was maintained, and a renewed Jewish population emerged in the Land of Israel. For reasons that are not at all clear, prophecy came to an end during this period. Prophetic figures did not appear—or at least, they are not recorded in the literature of the time—to remind the people of their obligations to God and to warn them of the perils of neglecting these obligations. This change, though obscured by the limited data from an ill-documented epoch of the Jewish past, was nevertheless clearly momentous. There are no texts from the period depicting God speaking directly to the people through emissaries. Instead, Jews were left with the written record of prior revelation to direct them, which like all such texts entailed a wide range of possible readings and interpretations. Explication of the biblical text became the new guide for Jewish living and thus the new foundation for educating Jews. This written record would serve as the basis for understanding the core dynamic of Jewish history as rooted in the covenant between God and Israel, for spelling out the demands of this covenant, and for promoting adherence to it.

The disappearance of the prophets and their replacement by explicators of the written record of revelation set in motion a search for new Jewish educational leadership. Deprived of their prophet/educators, the Judeans in the Land of Israel and Mesopotamia turned to a number of functionaries to fill the lacuna. In some ways, the likeliest candidates to fill the gap left by the disappearance of the prophets were the priests, who in fact did occupy a central role in Jewish leadership and as Jewish educators in the broadest sense for several centuries. However, the destruction of the Second Temple at the hand of the Romans in 70 ultimately deprived the priests of their favored position, one that had already faced some minor competition before the Temple era was brought abruptly to a close.

Slowly and over an extended period of time, the rabbis—whose claim to authority within the Jewish community was grounded precisely in their role as expositors of the Written Torah—emerged as those best equipped to clarify the demands of the covenant and to urge the importance of fulfilling those demands. The rabbis built upon the foundations already identified, chief among them the place of the covenant between God and Israel in Jewish fortunes. They were prepared to shoulder responsibility for identifying the obligations entailed in this covenant and for convincing their Jewish followers of the importance of fulfilling these obligations. In this way, the rabbis became in late antiquity the educators *par excellence* of pre-modern Jewry.

The rabbis approached their task with total acceptance of the dynamic of history as delineated so clearly in the biblical corpus. They absorbed fully the biblical view of human history in general and the history of Israel in particular. They focused heavily on the implications of this biblical sense of the dynamic of history. Indeed, they viewed the core of their leadership role as defining and elaborating in great detail the demands of the covenant and convincing their followers to fulfill these covenantal obligations.

Thus, with the passage of time, the rabbis replaced Moses and the prophets as the prime educators of the Jewish people.

The altered circumstances under which the rabbis lived necessitated minor tweaking of biblical thinking and some extension of the biblical paradigms as well. Biblical certainties were now viewed with a tinge of uncertainty. Armed with their belief in divinely imparted truth, the biblical author(s) of the Torah and prophetic texts portrayed Moses and the prophets explaining, with enormous confidence, specific instances of suffering as the result of failure in fulfilling the demands of the covenant. The rabbis by no means disputed the general view of the historical narrative, but were somewhat more circumspect in their assessment of specific instances of divine reward and punishment.

Well aware of situations that seemed to reflect the suffering of the righteous and the flourishing of the wicked, the rabbis made allowance for the limits of human understanding and the role of mystery in the divine-human relationship. This tweaking of biblical thinking was very much abetted by the development of conceptualizations of the afterlife. Reward and punishment subsequent to this-worldly existence offered the option of insisting on divine reaction to righteousness and sinfulness that could not be readily evaluated by human observers.

The extension of biblical thinking was related to the developing reality of substantial Jewish life outside the Land of Israel. From the Babylonian exile onward, the Jewish settlement in Mesopotamia remained a reality, although it left very little documentation for many centuries. As a result of the remarkable conquests of Alexander and his Greek army, the Land of Israel—situated at the eastern edge of the Mediterranean Sea—was increasingly dislodged from its Near Eastern moorings and became part of the Mediterranean/Western world. The early imperial rulers of the Land of Israel and its Jewish population had been Near Eastern—the Assyrians, Babylonians, and Persians—and the languages and culture of the Jews of the Land of Israel were Near Eastern as well. With Alexander, the ruling empire became Greek in one or another of its post-Alexander forms; Greek culture and mores, centered in urban areas, were increasingly influential among the Jews of Palestine. Then, by the first pre-Christian century, the Jewish community of Palestine fell under the sway of the Roman Empire, destined to rule it for longer than the Assyrians, Babylonians, and Persians combined.

With Palestinian Jewry's attachment to the Mediterranean world and eventually to the Roman Empire, the way was paved for new and voluntary Jewish population movement. Jewish enclaves developed throughout the eastern Mediterranean Basin and subsequently further westward as well. World Jewish population was thus spread beyond the Land of Israel in two directions. In the East, the well-established Jewish community of Mesopotamia remained firmly in place; in the West, a new Jewish diaspora emerged, with nodules all across the northern and southern shores of the Mediterranean Sea. The biblical narrative had focused on the Land of Israel as the promised and proper abode of the Jewish people. The reality of two healthy diasporas thus posed a theological quandary, which was resolved by the rabbis in the light of painful developments during the middle decades of the first Christian century.

Just as the earlier Judeans had rebelled against their Babylonian over-lords, so too did the first-century Judeans rebel against their Roman rulers. In both cases, the uprisings were harshly suppressed, with massive loss of Jewish life, destruction of the capital city, and razing of the central Jerusalem shrine. However, beyond these real and symbolically significant parallels, the suppressions of the two rebellions differed markedly. The most important difference lay in the fact that the Romans never adopted the Assyrian and Babylonian technique of punishing rebellion by exile. When the uprising of the years 66–70 was quashed and its suppression completed, much of the Jewish population of Palestine remained in place. Palestinian Jewry continued to constitute the largest Jewish community in the world. Indeed, Palestinian Jewry remained strong enough to mount yet a second rebellion against Rome in the year 132, a potent uprising that required three full years of intense Roman military operations to put down. It is with respect to the rebellion of 66–70 and its aftermath that the rabbis extended the biblical imagery of the covenant, the blessings for its fulfill-ment, and the punishments for its neglect.

In this eventual rabbinic imagery, the rebellion against Rome was pro-jected as precisely parallel to that against Babylonia. In both cases, the sacred city of Jerusalem was destroyed (which is true); in both cases, the central shrine of the Jewish people was razed (which is true); in both cases, the Jews were forced into exile (which is not at all true); in both cases, it was Jewish sinfulness that brought about the catastrophe (this is a theological assertion that cannot be empirically assessed and simplistically labeled true or false).

The rabbis as the religious leaders and principal educators of the Jewish people thus extended biblical imagery in major ways. In their view, the sin-punishment paradigm dominated both biblical and post-biblical Jewish life. Failure to fulfill the covenant had cost the Israelites of the northern king-dom their homeland and indeed their existence in the eighth pre-Christian century; similar failure had cost the Judeans of the south their homeland, but not their existence in the sixth pre-Christian century; parallel failure had cost the Jews of Palestine their homeland, but again not their existence in the first century. Indeed, the last of these purported exiles was fated to be far and away the longest, stretching seemingly interminably from the year 70 onward.

In the face of this extended sense of the biblical sin-punishment paradigm, the responsibilities of post-70 Jews were clear. They must seize on the Mosaic assurance of a covenant that was never to be abrogated, shortcomings and punishments notwithstanding. Jews living in the post-70 exile must attend to the comforting message of Moses, who told his followers that when "you take them [their painful travails] to heart amidst the various nations to which the Lord your God has banished you, and you return to the Lord your God, and you and your children heed his command with all your heart and soul, just as I enjoin upon you this day, then the Lord your God will restore your fortunes and take you back in love."[12] The way to good fortune was clear, and the rabbi/educators of the Jewish people took on responsibility for leading their folk in the direction of repentance and recommitment to the covenant, this time through Jewish study and practice.

THE EDUCATIONAL EFFORTS AND ACHIEVEMENTS OF THE RABBIS

In assuming their role as the leaders and educators of the Jewish people, the rabbis in effect undertook the two large tasks earlier shouldered by Moses and the prophets. They obligated themselves to clarify to the extent possible the demands of the covenant and to encourage their followers as vigorously as possible to fulfill these demands. Success in rabbinic fulfillment of these two functions would much enhance the prospect of individual and corporate Jewish wellbeing; failure in either or both would doom Jews living in what was projected as the punishment of the Roman exile to ongoing dislocation and suffering.

Clarification of the demands of the covenant began with intensive reading and explication of the written record of revelation, a core rabbinic function. The rabbis pored over the Hebrew Bible with excruciating care, seeking to glean every possible nuance from the texts. With the passage of time, as surrounding societies introduced new modalities of textual analysis, the rabbis adopted many of these techniques and made them part of their effort at extracting meaning from and attributing meaning to the biblical record. In its earliest stages, this project involved the effort to glean behavioral guidelines from a close reading of the biblical text. To be sure, such close reading resulted in more than clarification of behavioral norms; broader insights were produced as well, resulting in the elaboration of non-behavioral teachings from the biblical texts. Much of this latter effort was directed at convincing Jews of the importance of scrupulous fulfillment of the demands of the covenant. Both forms of reading the record of revelation—extraction of behavioral norms and development of broader insights—were maintained by rabbi/educators all through the ages as core pedagogical methods.

The process of clarification of the covenant and its demands through study of the biblical text for its fullest meaning resulted in a burgeoning rabbinic literature designated broadly as the Oral Torah, in contrast to the biblical Written Torah. The Written Torah was viewed as God's direct communication to humanity via Moses and the prophets. The Oral Torah was projected as the ongoing extraction of operative truths from divine revelation, through painstaking study of the biblical text and engagement of real-life issues with the biblical text. Significantly, much of the corpus of the Oral Torah emerged from rabbinical academies, where the primary focus was study and teaching.

As the findings of Oral Torah proliferated, the rabbis and their followers recurrently felt a need for amassing and organizing this expanding corpus in ways that would make it manageable and accessible. Thus, codification of the demands of the covenant emerged as a further modality of rabbinic clarification of the duties of Jews. The first authoritative code of rabbinic law was formulated in early third-century Palestine, in the Galilean academy of Rabbi Judah *ha-Nasi*. Possessed of wealth, recognized by the Romans as a political authority within Palestinian Jewry, respected for his own learning, and standing at the head of a group of distinguished rabbinic scholars, Rabbi Judah seems to have been in a unique position to organize and promulgate a collection of rabbinic laws that would be widely acknowledged as authoritative. The Mishnah produced in Rabbi Judah's academy became the first authoritative text of Oral Torah.

The dynamic of Oral Torah depicted thus far suggests, of course, an ongoing process and continued expansion of Oral Torah, and this was precisely what took place. The Mishnah became an authoritative text, which was in turn studied, scrutinized, queried, and expanded. Out of the Mishnah emerged two further authoritative collections of Oral Torah:

the Palestinian Talmud and the Babylonian Talmud. With the passage of time, the greater size of Mesopotamian Jewry and the superior reputation of its academies transformed the Babylonian Talmud into *the* Talmud, the new foundation for the subsequent study and expansion of the vast and ever-expanding corpus of rabbinic law. In all these ways, then, the rabbi/educators of the Jewish world fulfilled their first responsibility effectively: the responsibility for defining ever more precisely the demands of the covenant for the people whose fate depended on fulfillment of these covenantal demands.

Moses and the prophets, who preceded the rabbis as the leaders/educators of Israel, bore a second responsibility as well. It was their obligation not only to define and transmit the demands of the covenant, but also to alert their followers to the importance of fulfilling their covenantal obligations: that is, to communicate to them the blessings attendant on heeding God's call and the suffering that would result from neglecting that call. The emergence of the synagogue as the locus for human communication with the divine and the central role assumed by the rabbis in the synagogue set the stage for regular and meaningful communication of the importance of fulfillment of the covenant. In many ways, the synagogue—with its focus on words—was far better equipped for communicating this message than the Temple of yore had been.

The rabbis placed at the very center of synagogue ritual regular immersion in the biblical narrative and the prophetic utterances. In one-year or three-year cycles, Jews the world over recapitulated the sequence of stories that stretched from the creation of the world through early humanity, the Patriarchs, the sojourn in Egypt, the exodus, the wilderness wandering, the details of the covenant, and the closing exhortations of Moses. The underlying message of this saga, as we have depicted it, was thus regularly reinforced in the widest possible variety of places and times. These readings formed the centerpiece of the Jewish prayer service twice per week on weekdays, on every Sabbath, and on every special holiday occasion. Jews were constantly exposed to the core narrative of Jewish fate and thus the centrality of the covenant in their fortunes.

This core narrative and its unmistakable message were reinforced in two major ways. In the first place, the Torah reading for each Sabbath and every special occasion was supplemented by a further selection from the second section of the Bible, either a narrative passage or a selection from the prophetic utterances. As we have seen, the message of this second section of the Bible dovetailed precisely with that of the first. Thus, Jewish worship services throughout the year buttressed the message conveyed by the reading from the Torah with carefully chosen selections from the post-Torah writings as well. Repetition of the same passages year-over-year reinforced the messages over and again and progressively over the worshipper's lifespan. In terms of convincing Jews of the centrality of the covenant and its observance, the regular Torah reading was a highly effective set of not-so-gentle reminders.

The message of the Written Torah was reinforced in a second manner as well. From early on, the rabbis built on the biblical narrative through their synagogue-centered interpretations, expansions, and embellishments. Moses, in a way that is hard to imagine realistically, is portrayed as addressing the entirety of the Israelite people; the prophets clearly lacked a central venue for delivering regularly their message; the rabbis created precisely such a regularized vehicle for teaching the dynamic of history, for emphasizing the place of the covenant in history, and for urging their followers of the need for wholehearted fulfillment of the obligations laid by God on his chosen community. The synagogue sermon became a primary vehicle for the efforts of the rabbis to convince their followers of the necessity of fulfilling the demands of the covenant they were detailing and codifying.

We have no real sense of the establishment by the rabbis of a genuine educational system in late antiquity.[13] When such a well-ordered system was first made available for our scrutiny as a result of the rich documentation of the Cairo Genizah, its outlines accorded fully with what we would be led to expect from all the foregoing. Students were exposed first and foremost to the Written Torah, from which they were expected to glean the sense of the core dynamic of human and Jewish history, the centrality of the covenant in that dynamic, the major outlines of the covenant, and the impact of fulfillment or non-fulfillment of covenantal demands on Jewish fate. Advanced students proceeded to a study of the Oral Torah, with its further explication of the demands of the covenant.[14]

Over more than a millennium, the rabbis shouldered effectively their responsibilities as the educators of the Jewish people. They clarified in ever-greater detail the demands of the covenant in a variety of formats; they established effective institutional frameworks—including synagogues and academies—for convincing their followers of the importance of fulfilling the demands of the covenant; and they created a rich literature that conveyed their teachings throughout the Jewish world.

MAINTAINING CONSISTENCY UNDER EVOLVING CIRCUMSTANCES

Jewish understanding of the world, its workings, and the avenues to human wellbeing was remarkably stable from antiquity through the reorientation of Western societal organization and thinking that began during the Renaissance and Reformation and accelerated during the Enlightenment. Likewise, the leadership of the Jewish community charged with conveying this understanding and the educational settings in which their message was communicated remained stable as well, although this leadership evolved from those understood to have been directly chosen by God to those who took on educational leadership through their mastery of Written Torah and Oral Torah. This stability was enhanced by the organizational patterns of Jewish life throughout this lengthy period, patterns that conferred upon the Jewish community and its leadership considerable control of Jewish affairs, including Jewish education.

This overall stability is all the more remarkable given the extensive changes in Jewish life during this lengthy period. The diverse locales and environments in which Jews lived, the intellectual and spiritual quandaries Jews faced, the political and social challenges Jews confronted, and the internal structures for engaging these diverse circumstances all evolved markedly over time. That so much change could take place without disrupting radically the core assumptions of Jewish life, the leadership groups charged with transmitting these assumptions, and the educational structures within which the transmission took place is striking.

To be sure, the Jewish world vision was challenged over time by a number of widely embraced and potent alternatives. The first of these alternatives was the naturalistic and humanistic Greco-Roman world vision. From the time of Alexander's conquest of the Near East, large numbers of Jews were exposed in one form or another to Greco-Roman thought, with its sense of a world that operates according to relatively strict laws and that is immune to the reactions and interventions of the gods or even a God that purportedly created and ruled the universe. The challenge was formidable and required the rabbi/educators of antiquity and the Middle Ages to acquaint themselves with this alternative, to marshal convincing arguments for the superiority of the traditional Jewish worldview, and to seek ways in which aspects of Greco-Roman civilization might be introduced into Jewish life without detracting from core Jewish convictions.

With the passage of time, the Jewish vision of the world as created and controlled by one God was embraced and extended by two further monotheistic faiths: Christianity and Islam. Both these new monotheisms accepted the traditional Jewish sense of one God that created and controls the universe and a unique covenant with one human partner community. The first of these convictions made all three monotheisms respectful of one another, to an extent; the second ultimately entailed denigration of the other two as deficient. The opposition posed by these two subsequent monotheisms, with their larger numbers and seemingly greater success, posed a new challenge to the rabbi/educators of the Jewish people. Once again, the rabbis had to acquaint themselves with alternative and hostile views in order to perform their educational task fully. The seemingly inferior place of Judaism within the constellation of Western monotheisms had to be clarified and explained. These explanations had to be shared with the Jewish community in its entirety, so that Jews would never lose faith in their unique role in the covenant and the cosmos.

Jews continued to hold fast to their core convictions as to the existence of one God, the workings of the universe and history, and their special role in the covenant with the one and only God. This stability of belief was attributable in part to the power of the biblical vision, and in part to the capable leadership of the rabbis and the effective educational system they created. In addition, the organizational structure of pre-modern Western societies played a significant role. Pre-modern Western societies were organized in units: geographic units, social units, economic units, and religious units. Each enjoyed considerable authority over its constituents, and the Jewish community as a separate unit enjoyed such power as well.

Indeed, for almost all their history, Jews lived in semi-autonomous communities within larger polities. Genuine Jewish independence lasted for only a few centuries, from entry into Canaan until the Assyrian march westward. From that point (in the late eighth pre-Christian century) on, Jews in the Land of Israel lived in a semi-autonomous community embedded with a larger empire (Assyrian, Babylonian, Persian, Greek, Roman, or Muslim). Diaspora Jews for the entirety of their history lived under the same arrangements. What this meant in practice is that, from early times, Jews were accustomed to creating effective agencies of self-government. Increasingly important in this complex of agencies were autonomous Jewish educational institutions.

This style of Jewish self-governance extended far beyond imperial antiquity; it was characteristic of the Middle Ages and early modernity as well, down through the dramatic changes of the late eighteenth century. In the realms of both medieval and early modern Islam and medieval and early modern Christendom, the state operated as a collection of separate and semi-autonomous entities, each accorded considerable control of its own internal workings. During the Middle Ages and the early modern centuries, religious communities were among those entities. For the rulers of both Muslim and Christian states, the Jews constituted an identifiable and significant element within the corporate structure over which they presided. As such, medieval and early modern Jews—like their forebears in antiquity—owed loyalty and tribute, while enjoying extensive control over their own internal affairs. Jews raised their own taxes, had their own separate courts, and created independent social welfare and educational systems, operating with a very high level of internal Jewish authority throughout the Middle Ages and early modernity in the diverse settings in which Jews eventually settled.

The stability and consistency of the Israelite/Judean/Jewish worldview were in part the result of the persuasiveness and coherence of that world-view; at the same time, this stability and consistency benefited enormously from the workings of a powerful Jewish self-governing apparatus and from the influence that the leadership of this self-governing apparatus could thus exert over its constituents. How precisely did this self-governing structure work, and who wielded authority? While the answers to these questions were relatively (and surprisingly) consistent from the eighth pre-Christian century down through the eighteenth Christian century, evidence is full-est for the Jewish communities of the medieval and early modern world, and it was the organizational structure of these communities that shaped the closing stages of pre-modern Jewish life and that would eventually be dramatically disrupted as a result of the eighteenth-century reorganization of political life in the West along Enlightenment guidelines.

The self-governing agencies of the pre-Enlightenment Jewish world were grounded securely in three different sources of authority.[15] In the first place, there was powerful religious authority. In the Jewish religious vision, adherence to the dictates of the community and its leadership was a primary covenantal duty, indeed one of the most important in the panoply of Jewish religious obligations. This meant that recalcitrant members of the Jewish community, challenging for one reason or another the dictates of the communal leadership, could be appealed to immediately on religious grounds. They could be and were regularly reminded—forcefully and often publicly by their religious leaders—that, in their recalcitrance, they were in effect violating a fundamental Jewish religious law. This claim afforded a strong initial foundation for bringing internal dissidents into line.

The second grounding for the authority of the communal leadership lay in the social realities of pre-modern Jewish life. The corporate structure of societal life altogether made the security provided by one's native community vital. Being excluded from that native community was anywhere from highly disruptive to catastrophic. The importance of such belonging established a potent foundation for the authority of Jewish leaders over their followers. Faced with internal dissidence, the leaders of the pre-modern Jewish community could use their sway with the rest of the community to isolate the dissidents. Excommunication was a frightful threat hanging over the heads of pre-modern Jews. Like all potent weapons, it of course had to be utilized sparingly. The danger in excommunicating members of community was always the possibility that those excommunicated might choose to abandon the Jewish fold altogether through conversion to the majority faith. This was a serious danger and necessitated careful and nuanced utilization of the powerful weapon of social exclusion. Nonetheless, the weapon was real, and, utilized sparingly and judiciously, it very much enhanced the authority of the Jewish communal leadership.

The third and most potent weapon of all was recourse to the non-Jewish governing powers. Recalcitrant Jews who resisted the dictates of their leaders faced the ultimate danger of being turned over to the non-Jewish authorities. These non-Jewish rulers strongly supported the internal authority of the leaders of the Jewish community for obvious reasons. Effective internal leadership meant a minimum of energy expenditure for the fairly rudimentary pre-modern government agencies and a maximum of stability and revenue. The rulers of pre-modern corporate societies required strong and effective internal leaders and provided the backing necessary for such strength and effectiveness. Dissident Jews could face the prospect of punishment at the hands of the non-Jewish governments that exercised ultimate power over Jewish life. Once again, this was a potent weapon that had to be used sparingly. The Jewish leadership was extremely reluctant to introduce non-Jewish rulers into the internal affairs of the Jewish community. This was a ploy that might occasion harmful complications. Nonetheless, introduction of the non-Jewish authorities provided a weapon, utilized sparingly, that was extremely effective.

These three foundations of communal authority—religious authority, the social realities of pre-modern Jewish life, and appeals to the non-Jewish governing powers—translated into considerable control by the leaders of the Jewish community over their followers. The basic beliefs of the Jewish religious system and the Jewish worldview were strongly buttressed by this control.

Who, then, were the leaders of the Jewish community that exercised this control? The answer to this question lies in two directions: those with religious credentials and those with material power, which in the Jewish community meant essentially wealth and influence. Let us begin with the former.

Our prior discussion of the Israelite and Judean worldview identified a major point of transition in the cessation of prophecy and the elevation of the record of revelation—the Written Torah—into the foundation for the religious thinking and behavior of the Jews. With this momentous shift came the emergence of a new style of Jewish religious leadership, composed of those whose credentials resided in knowledge of the Written Torah and the capacity to understand and interpret it wisely. Especially important in this proper comprehension of the Written Torah was awareness of changing times and circumstances. Since patterns of Jewish life had shifted over the centuries and Jewish life was likely to continue to evolve, the masters of the Written Torah had to be especially adroit in grasping the underlying principles of the Written Torah and their implications, in order to properly guide the adaptations of God's revelation to new circumstances. As we hinted at above, a new religious foundation was the sense of parallel Torahs: the Written Torah, which is the record of divine revelation up to the point at which direct divine-human communication came to a close, and the Oral Torah, which contains the evolving explication and expansion of divine revelation over the subsequent epochs of Jewish history. As a result of the Roman destruction of the Jerusalem Temple and the concomitant loss of function of the priesthood, the Pharisees/rabbis emerged as the authoritative explicators and interpreters of the Written Torah.[16]

With the passage of time and the ongoing expansion of Oral Torah, the leadership claims of the rabbis came to include full command of both the Written Torah and the burgeoning Oral Torah. The rabbinic claim to religious leadership in the Jewish community was ultimately grounded in the conviction that the rabbis possessed the ability to perform the role earlier fulfilled by Moses and the prophets: that is, to articulate for the community their covenantal responsibilities. Subsequent to the end of direct divine revelation, it was the rabbis whose command of the record of revelation and its evolving explication could guide the Jewish community in its efforts to fulfill the obligations entailed in God's covenant with Israel.

There was a second leadership grouping in the pre-modern Jewish community as well, a grouping whose authority was founded upon material power. Wealth conferred leadership authority in the Jewish community for several reasons. First and foremost, one of the keys to Jewish communal survival was internal taxation. Internal Jewish tax revenues assured the ongoing support of the non-Jewish authorities, which was of course crucial to Jewish wellbeing. At the same time, this internal taxation supplied the funds necessary for maintenance of the range of activities required for Jewish existence. The tax burden bore down most heavily of course on the wealthiest members of the community, and this burden translated into a leadership role.

At the simplest level, the wealthiest members of the Jewish community had at their disposal the threat of withdrawal. Displeasure with community attitudes and actions could trigger a decision on the part of a disaffected wealthy leader to relocate elsewhere, which would deplete the community coffers in devastating ways. In addition, the wealthiest leaders within the Jewish community tended to employ many of their less fortunate brethren, and this too conferred great authority on the elite of wealth. Finally, Jews had to relate effectively to the non-Jewish governments under which they lived. Jews with relations to the non-Jewish authorities thus played a central role in Jewish affairs, and it was the elite of wealth that was likeliest to have pre-existent and positive relations with these non-Jewish rulers.

In sum, the Jewish worldview that emphasized God's power and depicted history as the stage on which divine reward and punishment played out was well established among Jews and convincing to most of them in and of itself. At the same time, it was strongly reinforced by the various coercive powers at the disposal of the leaders of the traditional Jewish community.

THE JEWISH TRANSITION INTO WESTERN CHRISTENDOM

Jews have been a wandering people over the ages. For our purposes, one transition in particular is especially important to note. At the end of the first Christian millennium, Jews were still ensconced in the traditional centers of prior Jewish population: the rectangular space that extends from Mesopotamia in the east through the Mediterranean Basin in the west. At that point in time, Jewish population was heavily centered in the Islamic sphere. Perhaps 80–85% of the world's Jews lived under Muslim rule, with most of the rest of the world's Jews settled in eastern Christendom.

Only a tiny fraction of world Jewry lived in western (i.e., Roman Catholic) Christendom. By the nineteenth century, this distribution of world Jewry had been radically transformed; by then, 90% of the world Jews lived in western Christendom. Most of these Jews were settled in the northern sectors of Europe, where almost no Jews were to be found at the end of the first Christian millennium.[17]

This monumental shift in Jewish population was not sudden or dramatic. Rather, it reflected the broad changes that had taken place in the West during the second Christian millennium. Western Christendom, which in the year 1000 was the weakest of the religious-political blocs in the West, trailing far behind the powerful realm of Islam and eastern Christendom, surged to the fore, becoming by 1500 the dominant power bloc in the West and gaining further strength thereafter. The growing Jewish population of western Christendom was a minor byproduct of this accelerating dominance. The growth of the Jewish population was in part the result of the geographic expansion of western Christendom. As European Christians reconquered the Iberian peninsula, for example, significant numbers of Jews were added to Christian Europe. Less dramatically but more importantly, Jews were attracted to the surging power and opportunities of western Christendom. This is especially the case in northern Europe, where a new branch of the Jewish people—often identified as Ashkenazic Jewry—was created during the period between 1000 and 1500.

As a result of this process of transformation, the bulk of the world's Jewish population was found in precisely those areas in which the process of modernization (to be discussed in detail in the next chapter) would first unfold. However, already during the closing centuries of the Middle Ages, Jews, Jewish communal life, and Jewish education were deeply affected by the special circumstances of their new environment. The new environment of western Christendom and its northern sectors created new opportunities for Jews and posed difficult new challenges—challenges that had to be engaged by the organized Jewish community and its educational system.

Because of the growing preponderance of European Jewry on the world Jewish scene, the patterns of Jewish life in western Christendom were subsequently viewed in many ways as normative for Jewish life over the ages. Three central conditions of Jewish living that were the result of the new ambience of western Christendom (and especially its northern sectors) have come to be viewed as common to all of Jewish history: (1) Jewish economic concentration in moneylending and banking; (2) projection of Jewish malevolence in a series of irrational slanders; and (3) Jews as subjected to intense missionizing pressure by their monotheistic rivals. None of these projections was common to pre-1000 Jewish existence in the older areas of Jewish settlement under both Muslim and Christian rule; all three eventuated from the unique circumstances of innovative Jewish settlement in northern Europe; all three created new challenges for the well-established Jewish communal structure and its educational system.

Settled human communities are frequently resistant to the immigration of newcomers. This common human propensity was exacerbated in medieval northern Europe by the monolithic religious character of the indigenous population, which was thoroughly Christian. Thus, the immigrating Jews were doubly stigmatized: They were both newcomers and religious others. To add insult to injury, they were also viewed as the descendants of Jesus' primary enemies, responsible in fact for his crucifixion. Popular resistance to Jewish immigration ran strong in eleventh- and twelfth-century northern Europe. The success of Jewish immigration resulted from the desire of Jews to attach themselves to this exciting new venue and the desire of major rulers to attract useful urban settlers from the more advanced areas of the south.

The successes of Jewish immigration were marred to a significant extent by popular resistance, which expressed itself strongly in the economic sphere. Jewish immigrants were precluded from settling normally and diversifying economically. They came as merchants and largely remained merchants, until new economic options were opened to them by the Roman Church's aggressive anti-usury campaign of the twelfth century. As Church leaders embarked on an effort to purify Christian society, one of their major targets involved Christians lending to fellow Christians at interest. To the extent that this vigorous campaign was successful, a lacuna was created in the rapidly expanding northern European economy, and Jews were in a position to fill this lacuna, for while Christians were forbidden to take or give interest to fellow Christians, no such restrictions applied to Jewish moneylending.

Thus, ironically, the Church's anti-usury campaign had the unexpected result of opening a new, lucrative, and useful economic specialization for the newcomer Jewish population. This new specialization enabled the young Jewish community of northern Europe to expand and solidify itself; it also exposed these Jews to further animosity, since moneylending and banking were traditionally reviled occupations. Consequently, Jews were hated as newcomers, as religious dissidents, as descendants of the enemies of Jesus, and as moneylenders, which constituted a powerful combination and required the leadership of the organized Jewish community to undertake extensive outreach efforts intended to elicit the protection of the established authorities of church and state.

The concatenation of potent anti-Jewish motifs in northern Europe resulted in the creation of a series of anti-Jewish images fated for a long and devastating history. These motifs began at the simplest level with the notion of groundless and malicious Jewish hatred of Christians, hatred so intense as to eventuate occasionally in murder. The objects of this hatred were often portrayed as children, since the young are perceived to be free of any actions that might justify murderous rage, and alleged violence against them would arouse even greater sympathy than against adults. By the middle of the twelfth century, the notion of groundless Jewish violence toward Christians, especially Christian children, was reinforced by religious overtones. Thomas of Monmouth, in the English town of Norwich, claimed that a pure and innocent Christian youngster was killed by the Jews, in this instance in a manner that recapitulated the Jewish crime of killing Jesus, that is by crucifixion. The purported crime thus involved Jewish hatred of both Christians and Christianity. During the thirteenth century, the notion of religiously grounded murder conflated the Christian calendar and Easter week (with its imagery of the Crucifixion) to the Jewish calendar and Passover. Jews, it was alleged, killed Christian youngsters in order to utilize their blood for the Passover ritual. (This new twist in the murder allegations would remain an element in Christian mythology concerning Jews as late as the twentieth and twenty-first centuries in certain sectors of the Christian world.) These notions of intense and violent Jewish hatred of Christianity and Christians also gave rise during the catastrophic years of the Bubonic Plague to the claim that Jews had orchestrated the plague by poisoning the wells of Europe. Once again, these expressions of anti-Jewish animosity necessitated vigorous and multifaceted Jewish defense activities by the Jewish leadership.

The Christian environment into which Jews were increasingly attracted was aggressive in its approach to non-Christians. Classical Christian theory, adumbrated by the Church Fathers, insisted on safe existence for Jews in Christian society, but stipulated in return that Jews must inflict no harm on their Christian host society and articulated sympathetic and reasonable missionizing argumentation directed at Jews as a core Christian responsibility. As the material power of western Christendom grew, so too did its missionizing ardor.

In theory, the aggressive new Christian missionizing aimed at non-Christians was directed equally at Muslims and Jews. In fact, however, the primary target of this campaign was European Jewry, for two reasons. In the first place, Jews were far more prominent in medieval western Christendom than were Muslims. While there was a Muslim population in Spain, as a residue of earlier Islamic control of most of the Iberian peninsula, elsewhere in Europe Muslims were sparse to non-existent. In contrast, Jews were to be found almost everywhere in Christian Europe, at least until the late thirteenth century and the spate of expulsions that began at that point. Equally or more important was the significance of converting Jews. Judaism as an alternative interpretation of the selfsame covenant claimed by Christianity was in and of itself a reproach to the latter, and consequently the Christian desire to convert Jews was intense.

The Christian conversionist campaign that began during the thirteenth century was potent and multifaceted.[18] It included traditional arguments for Christian truth drawn from the Hebrew Bible, venerated by both Christians and Jews; utilization of the newly reclaimed philosophic tradition to prove the rationality of Christianity and the irrationality of Judaism; exploitation of burgeoning Christian knowledge of the Jewish Oral Torah to argue that the rabbi themselves, knowingly or unknowingly, espoused Christian truths; and a powerful argument from Jewish fate that projected the lengthy record of Jewish diaspora wanderings, small numbers, and diminished circumstances as conclusive proof of Jewish error in interpreting the covenant and the contrasting rectitude of Christian reading of Israel's covenant with God.

This intellectual and spiritual assault on medieval Jews took place in numerous venues. Most striking was the enlistment of the secular authorities that were the Jews' protectors to force Jewish attendance at missionizing sermons and contrived debates. Jews were forced to listen to Christian arguments first-hand. Jewish complaints that this coercion violated the guarantee of their right to live as Jews in Christian society were rejected by the authorities of both church and state. Jews, the authorities asserted, were in no sense being coerced into becoming Christians, for they retained fully the right to dismiss the arguments they were forced to hear.

The missionizing campaign set in motion among Europe's Jews was seriously intended to foster conversion and was maintained for many centuries. It certainly had its successes, but overall the leaders of European Jewry seem to have successfully erected effective defenses against the wide-ranging Christian arguments. Indeed, despite the prohibition of impugning the ruling faith, the leaders of European Jewry also constructed for their followers piercing critiques of Christianity.[19]

Paradoxically, the Christian missionizing campaign—despite its harmful intent and occasional successes—contributed in a substantive way to the maintenance of the traditional Jewish worldview. In order to protect their followers, the leaders of medieval and early modern European Jewry had to engage directly the Christian claims and rebut them effectively. In the process, the traditional Jewish worldview was reinforced. As often happens, adversity resulted in intensified resistance on the part of those subjected to it. For Jewish rabbi/educators and Jewish education, reinforcing the Jewish sense of religious rectitude and indeed superiority became paramount. This involved all the settings in which Jewish education took place: in schools, in the synagogue, and at home as well.

THE JEWISH WORLDVIEW MAINTAINED

Despite Jewish peregrinations and the changing circumstances of Jewish life, the Jewish worldview first formulated in ancient Canaan proved remarkably resilient and durable. This durability and resilience reflected in part the essential vitality of the vision itself. At the same time, maintenance of the Jewish worldview was reinforced by other factors as well. These further factors included the societal structures that provided enormous control of internal Jewish life to the leaders of the Jewish community all through antiquity, the Middle Ages, and early modernity; the reinforcement derived from the monotheistic and covenantal assumptions shared by the larger and more powerful monotheisms under which the Jews lived from the Middle Ages onward; and—somewhat paradoxically—from the assaults leveled by the Church especially, which necessitated thoughtful rebuttal and convincing reinforcement of the traditional Jewish worldview.

With the onset of new thinking about societal organization and intense questioning of the monotheistic view of human history in Europe during the seventeenth and eighteenth centuries, the traditional Jewish worldview was exposed to unprecedented challenges far more fundamental and serious than the earlier challenges posed by Greco-Roman culture and the competing monotheisms. When new-style societal organization became a reality in the late eighteenth century and thereafter in the West, Jewish self-governance and the control it provided over Jewish behavior and thinking were decisively lost. Western Jews were thus free to consider—indeed, forced to consider—the new views of human history and its causation that were becoming increasingly dominant in the West. With far less authority at its disposal, Jewish education—now stripped of its coercive powers—had to confront a challenging and appealing alternative.

NOTES

1. Translations of the Hebrew Bible abound and regularly reflect the perspectives brought to the task of translating. For the purposes of this chapter, we shall utilize the translation sponsored by the Jewish Publication Society of America—*Tanakh: A New Translation of the Holy Scriptures according to the Traditional Hebrew Text* (Philadelphia: Jewish Publication Society, 1985). The translators brought enormous linguistic, philological, and historical expertise to their efforts.
2. Genesis 22: 2.
3. Genesis 22: 15–18.
4. Deuteronomy 28: 20–24.
5. Deuteronomy 28: 25–34.
6. Deuteronomy 28: 64–68.
7. Deuteronomy 30: 1–5.
8. For discussion of the Deuteronomic History. see John J. Collins, *Introduction to the Hebrew Bible* (Minneapolis: Fortress Press, 2004), 181–279.
9. 2 Kings 17: 7–8.
10. 2 Kings 17: 13–18.
11. For Judean treatment of the northern kingdom, see Daniel Fleming, *The Legacy of Israel in Judah's Bible: History, Politics, and the Reinscribing of Tradition* (New York: Cambridge University Press, 2012).
12. Deuteronomy 30: 1.
13. Numerous claims have been made about the establishment of a rabbinical schooling system in late antiquity, but none of these claims is solidly grounded. Perhaps best known is the fairly recent Maristella Botticini and Zvi Eckstein, *The Chosen Few: How Education Shaped Jewish History, 70–1492* (Princeton, NJ: Princeton University Press, 2012). Their argument for an early Jewish schooling system is marred by an approach to rabbinic texts that is no longer sustainable. Botticini and Eckstein accept early rabbinic statements as totally reliable reports of reality, an approach that has been abandoned by serious researchers in the history of the Jews in late antiquity.
14. The first truly reliable description of an early Jewish schooling system is based on the remarkable medieval data available in the Cairo Genizah. See S. D. Goitein, *A Mediterranean Society: The Jewish Communities of the Arab World as Portrayed in the Documents of Cairo Geniza*, vol. 2, *The Community* (Berkeley: University of California Press, 1971), 171–211.
15. Robert Chazan, "Medieval Jewish Political Institutions: The Foundations of Their Authority," in *The Quest for Utopia: Jewish Political Ideas and Institutions through the Ages*, ed. Zvi Gitelman (Armonk, NY: M.E. Sharpe, 1992), 67–79.

16. The sense of this new role is strikingly captured in the fanciful talmudic tale of Rabban Yohanan ben Zakkai's escape from besieged Jerusalem and his request for an academic setting at Yavneh.
17. Robert Chazan is currently completing a book-length study on the historical peregrinations of the Jews, tentatively entitled *Refugees or Migrants: Jewish Population Movement over the Ages.*
18. For an overview of this campaign, see Robert Chazan, *Daggers of Faith: Thirteenth-Century Christian Missionizing and Jewish Response* (Berkeley and Los Angeles: University of California Press, 1989).
19. For the major lines of Jewish response, see Robert Chazan, *Fashioning Jewish Identity in Medieval Western Christendom* (Cambridge: Cambridge University Press, 2004).

BIBLIOGRAPHY

Botticini, Maristella, and Zvi Eckstein. 2012. *The Chosen Few: How Education Shaped Jewish History, 70–1492.* Princeton, NJ: Princeton University Press.

Chazan, Robert. 1989. *Daggers of Faith: Thirteenth-Century Christian Missionizing and Jewish Response.* Berkeley and Los Angeles: University of California Press.

———. 1992. Medieval Jewish Political Institutions: The Foundations of Their Authority. In *The Quest for Utopia: Jewish Political Ideas and Institutions through the Ages,* ed. Zvi Gitelman, 67–79. Armonk, NY: M.E. Sharpe.

———. 2004. *Fashioning Jewish Identity in Medieval Western Christendom.* Cambridge: Cambridge University Press.

Collins, John J. 2004. *Introduction to the Hebrew Bible.* Minneapolis: Fortress Press.

Fleming, Daniel. 2012. *The Legacy of Israel in Judah's Bible: History, Politics, and the Reinscribing of Tradition.* New York: Cambridge University Press.

Goitein, S.D. 1971. *A Mediterranean Society: The Jewish Communities of the Arab World as Portrayed in the Documents of Cairo Geniza.* Vol. 2, *The Community.* Berkeley: University of California Press.

The Jewish Publication Society. 1985. *Tanakh: A New Translation of the Holy Scriptures according to the Traditional Hebrew Text.* Philadelphia: Jewish Publication Society.

CHAPTER 2

The Crisis of Modernity

From antiquity through the early modern centuries, the traditional Jewish worldview and the educational structures that transmitted it remained remarkably constant, despite the extensive changes in Jewish life wrought by ongoing migration across the length and breadth of the Western world and shifting majority environments. This constancy, in large measure the result of the internal power of the traditional Jewish worldview, was at the same time buttressed by external realities, including the broad patterns of majority governance that accorded extensive control of internal Jewish affairs—Jewish education prominently among them—to the established leadership of the Jewish community. The almost complete domination of medieval and early modern Western societies by alternative monotheistic visions also served in part to reinforce the traditional Jewish view of a divine-human covenant, by challenging Jews to marshal arguments in support of the uniqueness and correctness of their special relationship to the one and only God in the universe.

From the end of the Middle Ages (generally identified as roughly the year 1500 CE) onward, these external supports for the traditional Jewish worldview and the educational system it spawned were slowly but inexorably undermined.[1] Starting in the late eighteenth century, new societal structures first established in two states—the young and weak United States of America and the venerable and powerful France—steadily became the

© The Author(s) 2017
B. Chazan et al., *Cultures and Contexts of Jewish Education*,
DOI 10.1007/978-3-319-51586-1_2

norm throughout western and central Europe and the entire New World thereafter. The new pattern diminished the role of religion in Western societies and eliminated all entities that stood between the rulers and the ruled, including the semi-autonomous Jewish self-governing apparatus. Diminution of the role of religion in Western societies opened exciting new opportunities for Jews, but also weakened the centrality of religion in Jewish life. Moreover, without the authority of the previously unified and coercive Jewish community, Jews had to create communal institutions that were entirely voluntary. Both changes—the diminished centrality of religion and the need for voluntary institutions—had enormous implications for Jewish education.

Simultaneously, the underlying worldview held by the majority of evolving Western societies also underwent transformation. The dominant monotheistic perception of the hand of God at work in the universe—shared by Jews, Christians, and Muslims alike—began to erode significantly. This prior shared conviction of a universe controlled by the one and only God was increasingly replaced by the perception of a universe that is rigorously and inflexibly ordered by immutable natural laws that can be understood effectively by human investigation and are not at all amenable to divine intervention.

The political and social structural changes were authoritative and definitive. The organizational pattern of Jewish life was transformed from a semi-independent and monolithic communal structure that was reinforced by the outside authorities, armed with extensive coercive power, and thus capable of enforcing a high level of uniformity within Jewish life into an entirely voluntary set of Jewish institutions with no coercive power whatsoever and thus incapable of enforcing uniformity on their Jewish constituency. While some Jews may have been distressed by these changes, there was no recourse from them. However, the alteration of the worldview was an individual matter and showed considerable variability within the Jewish community. Some Jews embraced the new Enlightenment perspectives; some rejected them out of hand; many sought median positions that would meld aspects of the old and the new.

In view of the totality of the structural changes and the individuality and variability of the intellectual and spiritual changes, we shall focus on the structural first and then proceed to the intellectual and spiritual. Both were of decisive significance for modern and eventually contemporary Jewish education and life.

REDEFINING THE ROLE OF RELIGION
IN WESTERN SOCIETIES

Western societies had long been organized along corporate lines; states were conglomerations of separate and relatively independent groupings. The central authorities acted in effect as ringmasters presiding over this collection of separate units, which might be geographically defined, economically grounded, or religious in nature.

As the Western world became overwhelmingly monotheistic, religious sub-groups became increasingly prominent, and a new issue was added to the prior concerns of the ruling authorities. Rulers began to focus on the proper behavior and beliefs of their society's dominant religious community, whose views they felt committed to upholding. In the process, the uniformity of religious behavior and beliefs within minority communities gained the backing of the ruling authorities as well. While not in any way committed to the religious perspectives of the various minority groups, supporting the enforcement of religious homogeneity and conformity became part of the authorities' broad oversight of these minority communities. Muslim and Christian rulers of the Middle Ages and the early modern centuries thus supported religious conformity in the Jewish community, and that support had significant impact on the Jewish educational enterprise.

In medieval Christian Europe, where the Jewish population was increasingly concentrated, there was but one acceptable form of Christian behavior and belief: that which emanated from the papal court in Rome and was disseminated throughout western Christendom. During the Middle Ages, the religious uniformity of Christian Europe was regularly challenged. In part, the challenges were grounded in the gulf between philosophic teachings and religious doctrine; in part, they were purely religious, flowing especially from a sense of the disparity between the well-organized, highly structured, and richly endowed Church and what seemed to many medieval Christians to be the simpler, less formal, and more spiritual teachings of Jesus. In the face of both these threats—philosophical and populist—the Church fashioned a highly effective alliance with the political authorities that resulted in the branding and treatment of dissidents as heretics and thus criminals. For many centuries, this alliance operated with great cruelty and great effectiveness.

By the end of the fifteenth century this system was under great strain, and early in the sixteenth century it disintegrated. The key agent of this disintegration was an Augustinian monk named Martin Luther. Strikingly, Luther did not advance innovative criticisms of the Roman Church; his critiques were rather standard. With Luther, the key innovation lay in the fact that the efforts to silence him, which had worked so well for so many centuries, now failed. As this evident failure became known, the religious uniformity of western Christendom was irrevocably shattered. A number of dissident churches quickly emerged, creating an entirely new set of problems for European society, flowing from an effort to maintain the old system of governmental backing for religious conformity when the societal homogeneity necessary for such conformity was crumbling.

The problematics of the new situation were felt both within and between European states. Internally, the ruling authorities, whether Catholic or Protestant, were faced with massive numbers of dissidents within the societies they ruled. Their efforts to continue to impose the kind of uniformity that had been the hallmark of prior centuries were doomed to inflict profound suffering and ultimately to fail. Although it took centuries for this to be fully recognized, internal uniformity was no longer achievable. Parallel dislocation took place in relations between states as well. The notion of ruling authorities serving their own true church against heretical fellow rulers had functioned effectively during the prior centuries, but was no longer an achievable objective. Nonetheless, seemingly endless warfare ensued, at enormous cost in lives and resources.

Under these difficult circumstances, voices began to emerge that questioned the long-dominant norms of European life, chief among them the accepted sense that political authorities bore responsibility for the religious rectitude and conformity of the societies over which they ruled. Thinkers during the seventeenth century articulated a redefinition of the relationship between state and church. John Locke and others like him proposed replacing the well-established conviction of the interlocking relationship between state and church with a separation of function and operating strategies between the two realms.

In this radically new view, the state was projected as the protector of the civil interests of members of society, which Locke defined as "life, liberty, health and indolency of body, and the possession of outward things, such as money, land, houses, furniture, and the like."[2] The prosaic quality of this listing is no accident. Locke wished to stress the quotidian nature of the state's responsibilities; it exists solely on the terrestrial level and is charged with responsibility for regulating the mundane relationships among human beings. But it is necessarily a mandatory institution to which all members of society belong, and it possesses extensive powers of coercion. In order to protect effectively the safety and security of members of society, the state requires these coercive powers, for without them it would be incapable of providing requisite protection.

In contrast, Locke depicted churches as voluntary associations that take upon themselves mediation of the relationship between humans and the divine. The precise nature of that relationship is fraught with dispute and disagreement, which was reflected in the increasingly evident multitude of conflicting religious visions and disparate religious communities on the European scene. For Locke, churches were voluntary groupings and should enjoy no powers of coercion. Church members should be entirely free to come and go as they might please, with no obstructions placed in their path.[3] Critical to societal wellbeing is acknowledgment of the divergent functions of state and church, and maintenance of strict boundaries between them—a viewpoint that represented total repudiation of the prior structuring of medieval European societies and the call to an entirely new political order for the West.

The innovative call for strict separation of state and church in many ways represented a major boon to the Jews of early modern Europe. To be sure, these Jews played no role in the agitation for change, nor were they even raised as an issue by those calling for change. The stimulus to alteration of the prior pattern of governance lay entirely in the religious fragmentation of the Christian majority on the European scene; revision of circumstances for the Jews was merely a minor byproduct of the broader call for change that was an ultimate result of the Protestant Reformation. But for Jews the change was of monumental significance.

To the extent that the call to separate state and church was implemented, Jews would be transformed from a disadvantaged religious minority, circumscribed by numerous and debilitating limitations, into equal citizens of egalitarian societies that incorporated a wide range of religious communities. The shift was perceived by many individual eighteenth-century Jews as liberation from longstanding servitude. The end to religious coercion by the institutional structure of the majority society also meant an end to coercion within the Jewish minority society and thus had enormous impact on the internal controls and institutions—including the educational system—that had so long dominated Jewish life.

THE NEW EGALITARIAN SOCIETY

The changes that began to materialize during the eighteenth century included much more than separation of church and state, although this innovation became the best known and most resonant of the changes. Less obvious but equally important was a reconceptualization of the organizational structure of the European state. The long-accepted sense of the state as a conglomeration of separate units gave way to the conviction that the state should govern its subjects directly, without the intrusion of intermediate entities. To take the example of France, which was the first of the new style polities in Europe: The old order featured a complex French state composed of separate geographic areas, separate societal classes, and separate religious communities; this fractured polity gave way to a state composed of one nation living under one common set of rules applied throughout, rules binding on all geographic areas, all classes, and all religious communities. In relationship to the state, the only salient categories would be citizen and non-citizen.

The Jews of France provide striking examples of both the old order and the new. Back in 1394, the French king had ordered once again the expulsion of Jews from France, and this edict—unlike previous decrees of banishment—was never rescinded. Thus, throughout most of royal France—where the edict of 1394 was still in force—there were no Jews prior to the French Revolution. Nonetheless, there were significant pockets of Jewish settlement in France, and the explanation for this anomaly lies in the corporate nature of the French state. As new territories were added to France, they were governed differently from "old France." Often, the political arrangements of the prior regime were maintained. Thus, as the area of Alsace-Lorraine was added to France, the Jews already settled there were permitted to remain within the newly appended territory. This permission in no way entailed the right to settle in "old France," however. In other words, two differing sets of rules were in place for Jews—they could live in new French territories but they could not live in "old France." Reflected in these strange circumstances were two prominent elements in the corporate nature of pre-revolutionary France: differing rules for separate geographic areas and for separate religious communities.

In the wake of the revolution, the corporate structure of France was dismantled, with major implications for the Jews and their strange situation. Alternative rules for different geographic sectors of France were annulled and special regulations for different religious sub-groups came to an end. Thus, Jewish citizens of France could no longer be excluded from any regions of the now unified French state. Jews immediately began to leave the confines of their prior habitation and flock elsewhere, especially to the exciting capital city of Paris, which quickly became and has remained the site of France's largest Jewish population. This freedom of movement was a key element in the Jewish sense of liberation.

Matters, however, were not at all simple. There were prices to be paid by the Jews of France for their newfound rights. The first was the abolition of the Jewish community structure that had been mandatory all through the prior history of pre-revolutionary French Jewry, small and limited as it was. The powers of this pre-revolutionary semi-autonomous Jewish self-government had been extensive and effective, and Jewish education had been structured for the entire community by the Jewish leadership. Now, in one fell swoop the traditional structure disappeared. All Jewish activities, including Jewish schooling, became voluntary and had to be financially supported by voluntary funding. The prior system of forced taxation, out of which the funds for Jewish education would be derived, was now gone. Funding had become voluntary, as had establishment of educational goals and techniques.

There was a second price to be paid as well. When the issue of Jewish citizenship was debated in the immediate wake of the revolution, there were very few voices urging that Jews be denied citizenship as a result of religious difference. There were voices raised against Jewish citizenship, however, largely on the grounds that Jews were not in a position to become loyal and contributing citizens in the new French republic. This argument was couched in multiple ways: Jews had no sense of loyalty to the French nation; Jews were in fact unfamiliar with the French language; Jews lived off by themselves; Jewish economic activities were very limited, in ways that were at best useless or at worst harmful. To grant citizenship to such people, it was argued, was to create a problematic and potentially destructive element within the new and young French state.

These arguments were met and overcome by the counterclaims of the advocates for Jewish citizenship, who advanced the classic liberal argument in an especially potent form. Given the opportunity, the liberal argument went, lagging human populations will take maximal advantage of their new and improved options. In the case of the Jews, this meant that all the negative descriptions of Jews and their current behaviors were accurate, but that opportunities for equality would translate into much improved and constructive patterns of Jewish behavior. In the case of the Jews in revolutionary France, this "traditional" liberal argument was given a special twist. The obvious deformity of the Jews (on this there was no serious disagreement between opponents and supporters of Jewish citizenship) was traced to the limitations imposed upon them by the earlier Christian majority. Thus, for the post-revolutionary Christian majority to use the Jewish deformities it had itself created to deny Jews citizenship would represent a double injustice.

The liberal argument in its especially powerful form won the day, and Jews were granted citizenship in the new and egalitarian France, although the debate was contentious and lasted almost to the end of the constitutional deliberations.[4] Throughout the course of the debate over the Jews, both sides agreed that in their present state Jews were retrograde and potentially harmful. The disagreement focused on the augurs for the future. For one camp, the detrimental aspects of Jewish behavior were deeply ingrained and would not change; for the other, winning camp, the problems that Jews posed would disappear with the grant of citizenship and equality and the lifting of age-old restrictions.

French citizenship was an enormous boon for the Jews of France, but it came with conditions. French Jews were granted citizenship with the clear understanding that they must prove themselves worthy of it by changing their ways. They must become loyal Frenchmen; they must adopt French language and culture; they must integrate themselves comfortably with their French neighbors; they must shift into useful and constructive economic activities. The non-Jewish majority of France understood well the demands that accompanied citizenship; the Jews understood these demands even better. Jewish life would have to change in order to merit the gift of citizenship that France had granted. As always, the key to such change lay in the area of education. The education of Jews now had to take place in significantly new directions, as we will describe shortly.

There is fascinating evidence of the insistence that French Jews change just a decade-and-a-half after the momentous grant of citizenship. Stung by reports of allegedly problematic Jewish behavior, Napoleon—who had in the brief interim become emperor of France—convened an assembly of Jewish notables, to which he posed a series of probing questions.[5] These questions addressed all the issues that had been raised during the debate over Jewish citizenship. Napoleon wanted to know if there were obstacles in Jewish religious belief that would impede Jewish loyalty to France, Jewish integration into French society, and Jewish productivity in the economic sphere. Some of the questions were relatively easy for the assembled Jewish notables to answer; some were quite difficult.[6] In all cases, however, the Jewish notables understood well the answers that were expected, and they provided them. Jews could and would become loyal and productive citizens of France. This assurance created a strikingly new objective for educating Jews: the formation of Jewish citizens of the French state. When Napoleon received the answers he required, which he understood as an authoritative consensus of Jewish leaders, he took the further step of convening an assembly of Jewish religious leaders, presenting them with the same questions, receiving the same answers, and (in an oddly premodern twist) presenting these answers as the rulings of an authoritative Jewish Sanhedrin and thus religiously binding them upon France's Jews.

The traditional separatism of Jewish education from the concerns of the surrounding society was at an end. The formal structures that undergirded Jewish education had been dismantled, and the overall objectives of the education of Jews had now been decisively altered. Jewish education was forced to take on the function of preparing Jews for their roles as productive citizens in a new egalitarian society. No longer could Jewish schooling focus almost exclusively on religious teachings; rather, secular education became a central aspect of educating the Jewish young. Whereas at one time the education of Jews was a religious endeavor first and foremost, Jewish religious education would henceforth be distinguished from the general education of Jews, which had a decidedly secular and pragmatic thrust.

RECONCEPTUALIZING JEWISHNESS

Pre-modern Jews had long constituted a separate people with a distinct religious faith. While both Christianity and Islam had broken all ties with any particular national community, the Jews had maintained the combination of peoplehood and religion. The corporate structure of pre-modern Western societies was congenial to this combination. The Jews were perceived and treated as a separate political/ethnic group and a separate religious community, and the combination posed no difficulties. With the establishment of a new kind of state, however, that combination became problematic. The new European states were to be composed of citizens who owed political allegiance to their state and identified with its ethnic characteristics as Frenchmen, Englishmen, or Germans, while at the same time being adherents of diverse religious communities—as Catholics, Lutherans, Anglicans, and Jews—who expressed their faith in multiple ways.

This bifurcation of identity—which was comfortable for Europe's Christians, who had no difficulty in identifying themselves politically and ethnically as French or English and religiously as Catholic or Protestant—was highly problematic for Europe's Jews. Over the ages, they had identified themselves as Jews in every sense: political, ethnic, and religious. They had long prayed for return to the Land of Israel and reconstitution as a sovereign nation, with a renewed national religious shrine in Jerusalem. Accommodating these identifications and longings to the new structures of

European political life and its demands was a very difficult task. Slowly and painfully, Jews in the western and central sectors of Europe gravitated toward acceptance of the mandatory bifurcation, since there was no real alternative. Increasingly, albeit with difficulty, these Jews began to define (or at least describe) themselves as members of a religious community devoid of political and ethnic identity and aspirations. They were Frenchmen or Englishmen, like their neighbors, but with a different set of religious beliefs and practices. In effect, Jewishness was narrowly redefined as a religious identity.

The combination of the dismantling of the prior Jewish communal structure, the demand that Jews accommodate themselves to eighteenth- and nineteenth-century European life and culture, and the requisite redef- inition of Jewishness as religious identity, imposed heavy pressures and great stress on Jewish life in western and central Europe. The disappear- ance of the mandatory internal Jewish authority, while robbing western and central Europe's Jews of the instrument of control that had served them well over the ages, had the virtue of allowing for much greater flex- ibility in dealing with the new pressures and stress. In effect, a multitude of Jewish religious postures could now be embraced, with no impediments imposed by an established Jewish authority. Jewish religiosity, which was the only legitimate form of Jewish identity in the western and central sec- tors of Europe, could be and was now expressed in a multitude of ways, ranging from minor tinkering with traditional Jewish ritual and prayer all the way to massive reconceptualizations of Jewish belief and practice.

Thus, the religious homogeneity of European Jewry, which had included conformity to the traditional Jewish worldview and to established patterns of Jewish behavior and education, dissipated. A variety of religious sub- groups emerged, ranging from highly traditional to radically innovative. While there was much conflict and debate among Jews about these various expressions of Judaism, there was no longer a Jewish authority that could effectively declare one or another Jewish view unacceptable or illegitimate. All religious stances were now potentially legitimate. Jews were free to define their Jewish religious identity in wholly new ways, and they did so. Differing patterns of synagogue ritual emerged, and many traditional Jewish lifecycle practices were altered or even jettisoned. Inevitably, the traditional Jewish worldview in its entirety was challenged as well.

Given the choice between identifying Jewishness as religious identity, which would open the way to citizenship in the new European states, and identifying Jewishness as national identity, which would foreclose citizenship, the choice was relatively simple for the Jews of western and central Europe, despite the difficulties involved. However, the alternative of identifying Jewishness as national identity did have great appeal in eastern Europe, where the possibility of Jewish acceptance into an egalitarian national state was remote. The empires of eastern Europe remained congeries of ethnic communities that increasingly began to harbor dreams of creating their own states. As a range of national movements took shape throughout these empires, the large Jewish communities of eastern Europe added their voices to the nationalist fervor as well.

A variety of Jewish nationalist movements emerged, drawing upon a rich background of prior Jewish national identity and aspirations but in a modern key. To be sure, in earlier periods Jewish national aspirations had been expressed in conjunction with Jewish religious identity. In the new Jewish national movements, the separation we have already noted lurked clearly in the background. The movements were by and large free of religious overtones, although imagery from the religious past could be and was regularly invoked. While the vast majority of Jews in the western sectors of Europe, where egalitarian states were gaining strength, opted to publicly identify as Jews by virtue of their religious identity, many Jews in the larger Jewish communities of eastern Europe gravitated toward identification as a national community—in both cases, deeply influenced by the new patterns of societal organization that had emerged in the non-Jewish majorities.

Jewish national movements adapted for their purposes the rich panoply of symbols and features of the Jewish past, including language, culture, and the potent imagery of a corporate Jewish future. The most successful of the nationalist efforts—the Zionist movement—had a further powerful symbol as well: the historic Land of Israel as the birthplace of the Jewish nation and its ultimate destination. To be sure, in the traditional Jewish worldview, return to the Land of Israel would be set in motion by God, in response to Jewish recommitment to the demands of the covenant. But the Zionist movement was thoroughly modern, and its understanding of the modalities of return to the historic homeland of the Jewish people involved the human scene and human effort, without invocation of divine assistance.

Each of the multiple redefinitions of Jewishness generated its own educational vision and agenda. Those Jews oriented toward continuation of traditional Jewish religious praxis and belief attempted to the extent possible to maintain the traditional objectives and techniques of Jewish education. Jews oriented toward religious change and innovation could hardly continue to educate in the traditional manner; much had to change and did change. New objectives produced new educational practices, such as the emergence of religious schooling modeled on the Protestant system in the new European states or the dual-curriculum schooling that was favored by Catholics. For those Jews who defined Jewishness as national identity—most prominently the Zionists—even more fundamental changes in educational theory, content, and practice were required. Most striking was the importance of the evolution of a national language for the national movements. Whereas Jews over the ages had tended to use the language of their environment for educational activities in the schools or beyond the schools, for the Zionist movement, revival and utilization of the Hebrew language became a critical element in all phases of the educational endeavor.

The changes called for by Enlightenment thinkers and first realized in the two major eighteenth-century revolutions provided great benefits to Jews who opted to remain part of Western societies. These Jews emerged from an era of secondary status and profound alienation from the European mainstream into equal citizenship and full participation in the vibrant new civilization of the modern West. The exciting opportunities opened up by these changes were economic, social, educational, and cultural, and Jews took full advantage of them all. Jews individually became major achievers in multiple domains and leaders in many fields of Western endeavor. But collectively, Jews lost the community structure that had enabled them to maintain a Jewish worldview and Jewish communal identity so effectively over the ages and in so many different locales. Jews, now citizens of egalitarian societies, were faced with the necessity of creating new organizational structures that could form the foundation for communal life and activity. These organizational structures had to be voluntary, had to be funded voluntarily, and had to be effective without creating a sense of Jewish withdrawal from mainstream society. The challenge was daunting.

RECREATING ORGANIZATIONAL PATTERNS IN WESTERN SOCIETIES

The most obvious grounding for the voluntary organization of sub-groups within the new states of western and central Europe and the New World was religion. Catholics, Protestants of multiple denominations, and Jews shared the negative experience of losing government support for their religious identity while simultaneously enjoying the positive development of loosening government limitations on their religious identity. Success or failure in voluntary organizing would be determined by the level of commitment of the individuals that made up each group.

One of the byproducts of all this change was a proliferation of Jewish religious denominations. This was a new phenomenon in Jewish life, set in motion by the loss of internal Jewish authority, the demand for integration of Jews into modern Western life and culture, and the impact of the new scientific thinking that was beginning to dominate the West. This fragmentation of Jewish religious identity intensified the difficulties in creating new Jewish organizational frameworks. Synagogues, which formed the simplest of the organizational structures for Jews identified as a religious sub-community, came in multiple forms; synagogues that could organize and represent the entire Jewry of one city or even one neighborhood were no longer possible.

Pre-modern Jewish communal organization had done far more than attend to religious needs; it had provided defense activities, social services, and a strong educational system. Modern Jews still felt the need for these communal activities, but recognized that they would have to be funded and managed voluntarily, and knew that they ran the risk of raising majority fears of Jewish separatism and lack of civic patriotism. To the extent that these activities were undertaken, the efforts had to be exquisitely sensitive to potentially negative reactions in majority society.

A fascinating example of this Jewish sensitivity is provided by the famous Dreyfus Affair in late nineteenth-century France. Alfred Dreyfus was a French Jew who was deeply committed to the ideals of Jewish emancipation and complete involvement in French society. Like other members of his family, he pursued the educational opportunities now available to Jews. Eventually, he pursued a somewhat unusual career path by becoming a career military officer. Serving in this capacity represented the fullest possible commitment to the French state and French society. Dreyfus served with distinction, although he recurrently encountered hostility from fellow soldiers not at all used to having Jews in their midst, let alone in their command.

In a strange incident involving transmission of French military secrets to German authorities, Dreyfus became the scapegoat. Although completely innocent, he was convicted of espionage and sent off to painful imprisonment. His innocence was proclaimed and his case pursued by members of his family and by sympathetic non-Jews, including the famous novelist Emile Zola. The Jewish community, however, was utterly unwilling to lend its support to the campaign to exonerate Dreyfus; it was fearful of the imagery of Jewish group loyalty and perceptions of a collective willingness to support a Jewish criminal. Ultimately, Dreyfus was fully exonerated—an outcome that the Jews of France welcomed joyfully, despite their reluctance to be involved in the effort.

The creation of Jewish educational facilities constituted yet another problematic aspect of the effort to recreate aspects of the pre-modern Jewish community under the new modern circumstances. On one hand, Jews were concerned with inculcating Jewish identity in their children; on the other, they were highly sensitive to the need to comfortably be a part of majority European society. Their European neighbors provided them with two models for Jewish schooling, the Protestant and Catholic examples mentioned above. Embracing the new definition of Jewishness as religious identity, most Jews followed the lead of their Protestant neighbors who had created settings for religious instruction in churches—religious education that would supplement the secular education they were receiving in state schools. Many Catholics, however, had opted for a more intensive educational experience involving setting up Catholic schools that provided both secular and religious studies in one venue. To be sure, the secular studies had to fulfill the requirements of the state, but the more thoroughly Catholic environment, it was felt, would be helpful in molding Catholic identity. While the majority of European Jews opted for the first alternative, a minority opted for the second.

All of the previously discussed external societal and structural developments irrevocably impinged on western European Jewish communal organization and identity.[7] But the Jewish worldview was also altered by the impact of modernity—especially with its implications for Jewish education, one of the most significant vehicles for transmitting that worldview. Jews had lost the communal structure that had largely shielded them from outside cultural influences, and they experienced considerable pressure to integrate into majority society and culture. Thus, modern Jews were exposed to and affected by major developments on the broader intellectual and spiritual scene. As Jews moved from their previously cloistered existence into fuller participation in Western society and Western culture, trends in Western religious thought were also absorbed by the Jewish minority.

Still, evolving and innovative Western thinking, for all its impact, was of course not imposed on Jews in the same way that societal restructuring and the public redefinition of Jewishness had been. Some Jews did reject the new thinking (as many Christians did), and others absorbed parts of it and ignored or rejected other parts. But the fact that many Jews wholeheartedly embraced the new Western worldview, in part or as a whole, required massive changes in the Jewish educational vision and enterprise—changes that the contemporary Jewish educational system has even today still not fully acknowledged and engaged.

THE MODERN CHALLENGES TO TRADITIONAL RELIGION

Modern Western thinkers have long been stimulated by the impressive advances in the sciences in describing and explaining a universe thoroughly subject to the laws of nature. To most of these thinkers, the key to exercising control over this well-ordered universe and assuring a better life for humanity lies in intelligent utilization of burgeoning scientific knowledge to improve human circumstances. Moderns have come to view human resourcefulness in responding to and controlling the natural world's predictability as the optimal path to human wellbeing.

As this approach to understanding the universe and improving human life emerged, it severely challenged—and for many, came to replace—premodern notions of achieving human wellbeing by pleasing God, who controls the universe, through observance of a divine-human covenant. The notion of an orderly universe governed by unchangeable laws directly clashes with divine manipulation of history in response to human behaviors. The new scientifically grounded perspective on the universe has thrown into doubt and indeed into disrepute many of the core beliefs and practices of the monotheistic traditions; it has led many in the West—Christians and Jews alike—to dismiss them outright.

To be more specific: The Hebrew Bible and the New Testament both identify the covenant with God and its fulfillment or neglect as the dominant factor in historical causation. To the extent that God's human partners fulfill the demands of the covenant, God will reward them; to the extent that they violate the demands of the covenant, God will punish them. This was the key to pre-modern monotheistic thinking about history and human fate, as we already have discussed. The new modern worldview spawned by scientific success and its implications diverged dramatically from the notion of a universe that God manipulates in response to patterns of human behavior. For many Jews and Christians, the clash of worldviews has meant the often painful abandonment of one or the other. The difficulty of seemingly needing to make such a choice has, of course, moved many people to seek some sort of accommodation that would enable maintenance of Jewish or Christian identity alongside espousal of the modern scientific worldview.[8]

The most extreme and conspicuous element in the traditional understanding of the covenant was divine intervention on behalf of the covenant community in the form of supernatural miracles. For many Jews and Christians, belief in miracles became a litmus test for whether or not one could accommodate both the pre-modern and modern worldviews. Both the Hebrew Bible and the New Testament are rich in miraculous events. These miracles—clearly represented as disruptions of the natural order— are regularly advanced in the Hebrew Bible as the basis for belief in the God of Israel. When Moses was first commissioned by God to lead the Israelites out of Egypt, he resisted on the reasonable grounds that neither the Israelites nor their Egyptian masters would accept him and his claims. God's response was to provide Moses and his brother Aaron with a set of miracles that would prove their divine mission.

Indeed, the entire process of the exodus from Egypt involved a sequence of miracles intended to prove God's powers and God's commitment to freedom for the Israelites especially. These miracles included differential developments among the Egyptians and the Israelites, intended to dramatically emphasize God's power. With the final plague—the death of the Egyptian first-borns and the survival of the Israelite first-borns— there could be no doubt that divine intervention undergirded the suffering inflicted on Egyptians.

For the Israelites, this message was immediately reinforced by the miracle that took place along the shores of the sea. The fleeing Israelites were seemingly trapped between the waters that lay before them and the Egyptian forces bearing down upon them from behind. Obliteration seemed to be at hand. What took place was again a differentiated miracle: The waters of the sea parted for the Israelites, who passed through in safety to the other side. But as the Egyptians made their way into the dry path that had been opened, God intervened once again and returned the sea to its normal state, inundating and drowning the Egyptian forces. God protected the chosen people, and its enemies were destroyed.

Throughout the rest of the wilderness wandering and indeed throughout subsequent Jewish history, these miracles were recalled as prime evidence of special divine care for the Israelite nation and later the Jewish people. Miraculous events were crucial to the Israelite and Jewish sense of the divine control of history, but they constituted only its most dramatic evidence. In a more fundamental way, the prophets and the Hebrew Bible narratives depict the divine-human covenant and its demands on the Israelite people as the key to all of history. History was not a naturally unfolding process; its most important mechanisms involved God, God's special people, and the covenant that links the two.

Christianity, which emerged initially out of first-century Palestinian Jewry, absorbed thoroughly the Israelite/Jewish sense of history as controlled by God, once again with miracles serving as extreme examples of divine intervention in the historical process. In the Gospels, the supernatural powers of Jesus play a central role, albeit in more limited and personal ways than in the group miracles of the Hebrew Bible narratives. Jesus heals the sick and feeds the hungry, largely through individual and personal contact. All these achievements reflect impressive supernatural powers. Jesus even brings the dead back to life, which is the most striking miracle of all on the individual level. Indeed, the ultimate miracle in the Gospel narratives is the raising of Jesus himself from the dead, in the wake of his crucifixion. Jesus' resurrection is the crowning miracle of the New Testament narratives and the grounds for subsequent belief in the truth of Christianity.

For modern Christians, who absorbed the new scientific spirit and who wrestled with its implications ahead of their Jewish contemporaries (who for a time remained somewhat cloistered), the notion of divine control of history ran counter to the fundamentals of modern science. The miraculous was especially problematic, because it presented in dramatic fashion the disruption of the natural order. The new scientific spirit transformed miracles from a core proof of Christian truth into an embarrassment and source of confusion. How might it be possible to remain a believing Christian while embracing fully the new and convincing scientific worldview?

A second major challenge to traditional religious thinking and the biblical narratives of both faiths emerged during the modern period—a growing skepticism as to the reliability of the narrative accounts (miraculous or not) contained in the Hebrew Bible and the New Testament. Acceptance of the inerrancy of these accounts was fundamental to both traditional Judaism and traditional Christianity. Questioning the reliability of these accounts began with modern approaches to the New Testament, especially the Gospels. Christian thinkers had long recognized inconsistencies among the Gospel narratives, but had insisted that the seeming inconsistencies were in fact not real—they were introduced into the divine record to test the ingenuity and belief of Christian readers. Slowly, these traditional convictions were challenged, and emerging Enlightenment biblical scholarship came to understand the Gospels as four disparate human compositions reporting the actions and teachings of Jesus of Nazareth.

Once the inerrancy of the Gospels was challenged, the normal range of questions applied to all human literary creations became relevant and appropriate: Who wrote the work in question? Who constituted the intended audience? What were the sources of the author's information? What was the overarching message the author intended to convey? These questions were initially applied to the New Testament (as they were being asked by

Christian scholars of the scripture that was more central to their own faith), but eventually—and inevitably—they were asked of the Hebrew Bible as well. For centuries now, critical approaches to the biblical corpus have raised serious problems for traditional Jewish and Christian belief and believers.[9]

The accelerating discomfort with the miraculous—and, more generally, the notion of a divinity that intrudes into the workings of the universe—as well as the growing skepticism about the reliability of the biblical record engendered a wide range of reactions among both Christians and Jews. For some Christians and Jews, these issues forced a total break with traditional patterns of religious thinking, leading in a number of different directions: deism, the notion of a God who created the universe and then left it to its own devices; agnosticism, a sense that nothing can be known about all these issues; and atheism, an outright rejection of any conventional belief in God.

Among Jews, increasingly integrated into Western societies and cultures, the doubts sown by the intellectual and spiritual challenges of modernity slowly but inexorably exercised considerable impact. As was true for the Christian majority, a sub-group within modern Western Jewry maintained steadfastly their prior worldview, rejecting entirely the modern doubts. At the other end of the spectrum of Jewish reactions to the challenges of modern thinking were Jews who broke decisively with traditional religious thinking, and in the process left the Jewish fold entirely.[10] Within the extensive middle ground between these two extremes, there were a number of moderate responses. For example, there were Jews who sought successfully to reconstruct Jewish religious thinking in ways that would obviate the challenges we have identified, much as there were Christians who reformulated Christian belief in ways that would enable them to remain religious Christians. On the other hand, there were Jews for whom the modern challenges disrupt traditional religious belief, but who sought and found alternative foundations for maintaining Jewish identity.

MAINTAINING A JEWISH RELIGIOUS WORLDVIEW

Modern doubts were by no means decisive for all modern Christians or all modern Jews. Both communities had considerable numbers of adherents who rejected totally the claims introduced by modern scientific thinking and continued to insist on the inerrancy of their sacred texts and on indisputable divine control of human history and human affairs. Such Jews largely distanced themselves (to the extent possible) from modern culture—living separately, maintaining their own educational system, and discouraging their young from any involvement in non-Jewish educational settings. This tendency was rather difficult to maintain in European societies, which, as we have noted, were insistent upon Jewish embrace of the mores of the national society as a condition of citizenship. (In America, with a more relaxed view of societal conformity as we shall shortly see, this kind of self-segregation was and remains acceptable, so long as it is not rendered obvious by a large number of self-segregating Jews.)[11]

At the opposite end of the spectrum of religious responses to the challenge of modernity was an emphasis on evolution in human religious sensibilities and the necessity of distinguishing between the essential and the peripheral in religious traditions. For such religious thinkers, there were core religious values in Christianity and Judaism and peripheral details that could be allowed to lapse. For the adherents of Christianity, a fascinating example of the latter can be found in what is often referred to as "The Jefferson Bible."[12]

Thomas Jefferson, a Founding Father of the United States and the primary author of the Declaration of Independence, wrestled with the dilemma created by the modern challenges to traditional religiosity and produced a striking response. For Jefferson, the truth of Christianity lay in the elevated moral behavior and teachings of Jesus of Nazareth. This moral behavior and instruction serve as the essence of Christian faith. The ideals exemplified and taught by Jesus constitute the most penetrating insight into the moral dimension of nature. The behaviors taught by Jesus do not shape the course of history by evoking the support and intervention of God, who then bends history in the direction of faithful Christians. Rather, those behaviors represent the profoundest possible illumination of the moral order of the universe. Those who live by these teachings prosper; those who disregard these teachings suffer. Their success and failure do not reflect the hand of God in the world, but rather the irresistible workings of the universe. Jesus is thus transformed from a supernatural being into a purveyor of brilliant insights into both the moral order of the universe and the human behavior patterns that are in consonance with that moral order and thus assure a blessed life. The promulgation of these dazzling insights might be designated divine inspiration, but it might alternatively be labeled a remarkable human achievement. The former view maintains an element of the supernatural; the later dispenses with it.[13]

Jefferson thus addressed the two major challenges posed to traditional religiosity by modern thinking. For him, insisting on the divine roots of the Gospel accounts of Jesus is not necessary to recognize the brilliance of the insights attributed to him. More strikingly, the truth of Christianity thus had no need of the problematic baggage of the miraculous. Jefferson's Bible was composed of Jesus' moral behaviors and teachings, stripped of the complications introduced by miracles; there was no birth of Jesus to a virgin, no raising of the dead by Jesus, and no resurrection of Jesus himself. The elevated nature of Jesus' behavior and his teachings served as the utterly convincing evidence of the truth of the faith he founded. In effect, Jefferson was able to fuse the new scientific worldview with Christianity, although the Christianity involved was hardly traditional.

The Jews of the modern West faced the same challenges—albeit with some time lag—and came up with responses that in many senses paralleled those of their Christian neighbors. Many Jews—especially those attracted to the reforming religious movements in the now diversified Jewish community—deemphasized the biblical narratives and focused instead on the ethical teachings of ancient Israel as adumbrated in the prophetic books of the Hebrew Bible. In much the same way as Thomas Jefferson focused on the ethical and moral teachings of Jesus, these Jewish thinkers focused on the ethical and moral imperatives articulated by Isaiah, Jeremiah, and their prophetic peers. Prophetic emphasis on social justice, concern for the wellbeing of the downtrodden, and advancing the cause of peace in human society was put forth as the core value of Judaism and a reflection of the abiding truth and richness of the Israelite and subsequently Jewish religious tradition.

To be sure, the prophets of Israel had depicted these teachings as the key to Israelite success or failure, but reforming Jewish thinkers embracing the scientific worldview—in much the same way as Jefferson had—rejected this cause-and-effect claim. The visions of Isaiah, Jeremiah, and their prophetic peers were simply glorious and true for all times in and of themselves. Societies that neglected the prophetic demands suffered, but not at the hands of an angry God. Rather, neglecting these profound religious truths leads to human self-destruction. Put differently, the prophets could comfortably be viewed as providing a thoroughly naturalistic and at the same time spiritually brilliant perspective on human affairs. While these prophets spoke in the theistic language of their times, their utterances could be readily reinterpreted in a thoroughly modern idiom.

A Jewish perspective on change, preserving the essential and discarding the peripheral, was well expressed by an early Reform Jewish thinker, the Hungarian Rabbi Aaron Chorin:

> If we show ourselves as ready to strip off these unessential additions which often forced themselves upon our noble faith as the spawn of obscure and

dark ages and if we are determined to sacrifice our very lives for the upholding of the essential, we will be able to resist successfully with the help of
God all wanton, thoughtless, and presumptuous attacks which license or
ignorance may direct against our sacred cause.[14]

This sense of accretions imposed during prior "dark ages" and no longer consonant with enlightened modern thinking and the need to efface
them was shared by religious reformers both Christian and Jewish. Both
groups aroused intense anger among traditionalists, for whom the changes
represented human arrogance and unacceptable alteration of divinely
revealed truth. In the Jewish world, the war of words between the traditionalists and the reformers was protracted and intense, with charges and
countercharges flying throughout Europe.

There was also, to be sure, a moderating element in modern European
Jewish society—a group deeply devoted to traditional Jewish praxis yet open
to many elements of modern thinking. These Jews rejected both the traditionalists' rigid rejection of modernity and the willingness of the reformers to
introduce radical change in practice and reject God's role in history. A major
figure in this centrist path was Rabbi Samson Raphael Hirsch, who called
for respect for the tradition combined with openness to the modern world:

> Our aims also include the conscientious promotion of education and cul-
> ture, and we have clearly expressed this in the motto of our Congregation:
> An excellent thing is the study of Torah combined with the ways of the
> world [*Yafeh talmud torah im derekh eretz*]—thereby building on the same
> foundations as those which were laid by our sages of old.[15]

For Hirsch and his followers, they were not innovators in their openness
to modernity; they were merely following in the footsteps of their venerated ancestors.

This new fragmentation of Jewish religious beliefs and attitudes had
been made possible by the dismantling of the earlier authoritarian Jewish
communal structure. In the absence of a governmentally backed, unified
Jewish communal leadership, a wide range of groupings could proclaim
themselves the proper interpreters of Judaism without any authoritative
voice to declare one or the other grouping illegitimate. As John Locke had
urged his fellow citizens centuries earlier, there was no longer coercion in
the sphere of religion. The implications of the resulting fragmentation and
the alternative directions for Jewish education and life ultimately put forth
by the differing Jewish religious groupings were clearly enormous.

ADAPTING TO THE NEW: THE HISTORIC ACHIEVEMENTS
OF THE JEWISH PEOPLE

As many Europeans became increasingly dubious about or dismissive of the supernatural, alternative groundings for identity gravitated toward the natural. Many Christians began to abandon their sense of Christian greatness rooted in God's choice of the Church and of English, French, or German distinction likewise rooted in divine selection. Instead, they began to render the greatness of their faith and their nation in terms of human achievement. Once again, as Jews came late to the growing recoiling from supernatural understandings of faith, they had models from which to draw.

Making the case for the richness of the Jewish past, however, involved a new approach to Jewish history. Some prior predispositions, within both the majority culture and Jewish culture, had to be resisted. One of these was the traditional Christian negativity toward the Jewish past; another was the negative Jewish view of the Jewish past. Both views were grounded in the traditional Israelite/Jewish legacy that depicted history as the setting in which divine approbation or dissatisfaction played out.

For Christians, Jews had sinned monumentally in rejecting Jesus and causing his death. This sinfulness resulted in more than simply punishment; in the Christian view, Jewish sinfulness eventuated in annulment of the covenantal relationship between God and the Jews and replacement of the latter by the Church. Thus, punishment of the Jews in the Church's view was to be intense and ongoing and would conclude only at the point when Jews might join the true faith.

The traditional Jewish view of Jewish history was less negative, but only slightly so. Traditional Jews subscribed to the same sense of the dynamic of history, to the same conviction of Jewish sinfulness (although the sins were not readily specifiable and certainly had nothing to do with Jesus), and to the same general conclusion that God had imposed punishment on his errant people (although for Jews the punishment was not intended to be interminable). Differences notwithstanding, traditional Jews viewed the post-70 CE history of the Jews as, among other things, an uninterrupted sequence of deserved catastrophes. Jettisoning this perspective required a sea change in approaching the Jewish past.

The earliest stage in this revisioning of the Jewish past was associated with the drive for equal rights as citizens and the need to counteract the negative views of Jews that were current in European societies. Given the sense in some non-Jewish quarters that Jews were unfit for citizenship and the further conviction that they would be incapable of change in view of their lengthy history of negative behaviors, some Jews set out to reexamine the Jewish past from a fresh perspective. The first step in adopting a fresh perspective involved abandonment of the theological views of both the Christian majority and the Jewish minority, which highlighted Jewish shortcomings. However, the alternative could hardly be replacement of one set of prejudgments (negative) with another set of prejudgments (positive).

By the nineteenth century, the new scientific spirit we have identified had come to exercise a significant impact on historical thinking. The commitment to "scientific" study of the human past had emerged, along with the procedures for achieving this objective. The first step in achieving an objective rendering of the human past required rejection of all prejudgments. The next involved the collection of the most complete set of data possible. Just as research in the natural sciences began with scrupulous collection of the broadest possible evidence, so too in constructing "scientific" history, the key was identification and collection of rich data. The data could not be selective; they had to be scrupulously comprehensive. Materials long neglected out of a sense of their insignificance had to be brought into play. At the point that a rich and comprehensive set of sources had been created, a responsible and objective history could then be undertaken.

Within western European Jewry, a group of young Jews committed themselves to this project. They envisioned their undertaking unfolding in three stages: the data-collection stage; the writing of a series of histories of Jewish communities in diverse places and alternative time periods (in recognition of the extensive demographic shifts in the Jewish past that we have noted); and the identification of major characteristics of the Jewish people.[16] Over the past two centuries, the first two stages in this process have been zealously pursued, with remarkable success. Enormous quantities of source materials, bequeathed both by Jews and by their non-Jewish contemporaries, have been amassed and analyzed, resulting in relatively reliable histories of a wide range of Jewish communities. Paradoxically, these successes have rendered achievement of the third stage of the project—distillation of the essence of the Jewish past—unachievable. The more that knowledge of the diversity of the Jewish past has come to the fore, the more remote the objective of distilling any monolithic essence of the Jewish past has become.

In the early stages of the modern and "scientific" study of Jewish history, ulterior motives were quite clear. Fuller and better knowledge of the Jewish past would convince both non-Jews and Jews of the riches of that past and would, in the process, alter negative pre-conceptions about

Jews and Judaism among both non-Jews and Jews. Let us note one conspicuous example of success in that direction. As the issue of citizen rights for Jews was debated in late-eighteenth- and nineteenth-century Europe, there was agreement among non-Jewish observers and even among many Jews that Jewish intellectual abilities were focused on the practical, and that Jews historically had shown no propensity whatsoever for scientific or philosophic thinking or for aesthetic creativity.

However, the new investigators of Jewish history, as they ransacked the libraries of Europe in search of augmented data for reconstructing the Jewish past, unearthed a treasure trove of medieval Jewish scientific and philosophic writings. The figure of Moses Maimonides alone—a distinguished twelfth-century Jewish physician and medical researcher and a profound philosopher and theologian—refuted the imagery of Jews as lacking scientific or philosophic aptitude. As archeological investigation of the ancient Near East progressed, which constituted yet another modality of expanding the data for reconstructing the Jewish past, the sense of the Jews as aniconic, rigorously opposed to artistic imagery, and completely lacking aesthetic skills and sensitivity also gave way. Non-Jews could no longer confidently speak of inherent limitations in the Jewish cultural repertoire. Equally important for Jews as well—many of whom were caught up in the modern struggle to maintain their Jewish identity—the new data upset negative pre-conceptions of their own heritage. Simplistic generalizations about the Jewish past and Jewish capacities were rebutted, which was precisely the objective of many of those involved in the new Jewishly sponsored research.

Given the erosion of the supernatural foundations of modern Jewish identity, this new scientific (and more positive) sense of the Jewish past offered another way of retaining Jewish identity without recourse to traditional and increasingly problematic supernaturalism. Without necessarily invoking God and divine intervention in history, modern Jews could take pride in and identify with the heritage of their people.

In his influential survey of Jewish memory and Jewish history, *Zakhor*, historian Yosef Hayim Yerushalmi dealt at length with this recent turn to the Jewish past as grounding for Jewish identity. After analyzing the place of the traditional theological scheme in pre-modern Jewish memory, Yerushalmi turns his attention in the final chapter to the modern phenomenon we have depicted. According to Yerushalmi, the circumstances of modernity have created an altered and augmented role for history in modern Jewish life: "For the first time it is not history that must prove its utility to Judaism, but Judaism that must prove its validity in history, by revealing and justifying itself historically."[17] In this vein, Yerushalmi introduces a striking description of modern historically oriented Jews, advancing a felicitous phrase that has subsequently resonated widely.

> The modern effort to reconstruct the Jewish past begins at a time that witnesses a sharp break in the continuity of Jewish living and hence also an ever-growing decay of Jewish group memory. In this sense, if for no other, history becomes what it had never been before—the faith of fallen Jews.[18]

History as "the faith of fallen Jews" has proven a popular slogan among Jewish scholars and lay readers ever since.[19] While we agree fully with Yerushalmi's analysis of changing Jewish attitudes toward Jewish history, we much prefer the formulation of history as the faith of *modern* Jews.

NEW EDUCATIONAL PERSPECTIVES AND CULTURES

The realization of Enlightenment ideals beginning with the great revolutions of the late eighteenth century radically altered the settings within which Jewish education takes place, the leadership of the enterprise, and its orientations. No longer living in semi-autonomous communities with authority conferred on the traditional religious leadership, Jews have had to create new and voluntary settings for Jewish education. In western and central Europe, these settings were by and large synagogue-based, as Jewishness was equated with religious identity by the non-Jewish majority and the Jewish minority. The new educational venues came in multiple versions, since the separation of church and state as enacted within the Jewish community resulted in a multiplicity of Jewish religious denominations and points of view.

As Jews encountered the opportunity and indeed the obligation of involving themselves in the intellectual life of majority society, they necessarily imbibed the Enlightenment critiques of traditional religion. These critiques, and the creative alternatives they spawned, complicated the Jewish educational enterprise considerably. Breaking with the traditional worldview and its educational implications was of course daunting, but avoiding the search for new modalities of Jewish identity and the educational practices that might support them would have meant abandoning modern Jews to two stark choices: accepting the traditional Jewish worldview and its educational approaches or abandoning the Jewish fold altogether. Fortunately, many modern Jews rejected these limited options and sought instead new ways of identifying as Jews and new ways of educating their peers and off-spring toward these new forms of Jewish identification.

Inevitably, an alteration of the traditional vision of Jewishness also involved substantial and innovative changes in the culture of Jewish edu-cation. The new environment in which modern Jews found themselves necessitated new settings for and new styles of educational activity, with much of the new Jewish educational culture borrowed from the evolving majority context. These new settings and styles were readily adopted by those seeking educational modalities that would be useful in reinforcing the Jewishness of modern Jews, both young and old.

There were many new challenges—both general and specifically edu-cational—common to all modern Jewish communities, but there were significant differences as well. As we shall see in the following chapter, the unique circumstances provided by the newly formed United States of America and the special unfolding of Jewish history in the young republic created unique opportunities for modern Jewish identity formation and innovation in Jewish education.

NOTES

1. The precise boundaries between the medieval and the modern are prob-lematic. The medieval period is usually projected as ending with the fif-teenth century, for a number of reasons. The French *Annales* school—very much focused on broad historical developments and change—prefers to project a longer Middle Ages, which concluded with the end of the eigh-teenth century and the reorganization of European societies. This latter view fits well with the pattern of change in European Jewish life we are noting here.
2. John Locke, *A Letter Concerning Toleration* (Amherst, NY: Prometheus Books, 1990), 18.
3. For Locke's treatment of churches, see ibid., 22–36.
4. For key sources in this debate and its resolution, see Paul Mendes-Flohr and Jehuda Reinharz, *The Jew in the Modern World: A Documentary History* (New York: Oxford University Press, 2010), 123–28.
5. For the key sources on the Napoleonic call for an Assembly of Jewish Notables and the subsequent Sanhedrin, see ibid., 148–59.
6. Especially difficult were the questions about Jewish law distinguishing between lending at interest to Jews and to non-Jews and about Jewish law and intermarriage.

7. While we have noted the redefinition of Jewishness as religion in the western and central sectors of Europe and as national identity in eastern Europe, we shall henceforth focus only on the issues of Jewish identity and education in the new egalitarian societies in which Jews were identified primarily as a religious community. As noted in the next chapter, America has provided an unusual level of flexibility for Jewish identity, which has opened new educational options for America's Jews.

8. To be sure, the intrusion of naturalistic perspectives was not entirely new in the Jewish world. Medieval Jews, from the twelfth century on, were from time to time impacted by reemergent Aristotelian naturalism, and major Jewish intellectuals, beginning with Maimonides, embraced these views in areas like the nature of the cosmos and the dynamics of history. However, these Jewish intellectuals were careful to write for each other only and to shield the broad Jewish populace from their views by writing in a deliberately opaque way. For a fascinating example of such speculation, see Adrian Sackson, "Rationalistic Messianism and the Vicissitudes of History: The Final Chapter of Joseph Ibn Kaspi's *Tam ha-Kesef*," *Zutot: Perspectives on Jewish Culture* 12 (2015): 1–15. This protective stance of the medieval Jewish intellectuals disappeared with the broad modern Jewish acceptance of the new naturalism.

9. These same questions are slowly and painfully being raised with respect to the Quran.

10. Such Jews could of course find a place in the Jewish nationalist groupings, for which religious issues were essentially irrelevant.

11. See below, Chap. 3.

12. Thomas Jefferson, *The Jefferson Bible: The Life and Morals of Jesus of Nazareth* (Boston: Beacon Press, 1989).

13. Precisely where Jefferson stood on this spectrum is a matter of considerable disagreement. On these issues, see Matthew Stewart, *Nature's God: The Heretical Origins of the American Republic* (New York: Norton, 2014).

14. Mendes-Flohr and Reinharz, *The Jew in the Modern World*, 211.

15. Ibid., 222.

16. For some of the early formulations of this campaign, see ibid., 236–56.

17. Yosef Hayim Yerushalmi, *Zakhor: Jewish History and Jewish Memory* (Seattle: University of Washington Press, 1982), 84. For extended observations on *Zakhor* and the place of Jewish history in modern Jewish identity, see Robert Chazan, "From Jewish Memory to Jewish History: *Zakhor* Revisited," to appear in the *Journal of Jewish Thought and Philosophy*.

18. Yerushalmi, *Zakhor*, 86.

19. David Myers and Alexander Kaye, eds., *The Faith of Fallen Jews: Yosef Hayim Yerushalmi and the Writing of Jewish History* (Waltham, MA: Brandeis University Press, 2014).

BIBLIOGRAPHY

Chazan, Robert. forthcoming. From Jewish Memory to Jewish History: *Zakhor* Revisited. *Journal of Jewish Thought and Philosophy*.

Jefferson, Thomas. 1989. *The Jefferson Bible: The Life and Morals of Jesus of Nazareth*. Boston: Beacon Press.

Locke, John. 1990. *A Letter Concerning Toleration*. Amherst, NY: Prometheus Books.

Mendes-Flohr, Paul, and Jehuda Reinharz. 2010. *The Jew in the Modern World: A Documentary History*. 3rd ed. New York: Oxford University Press.

Myers, David, and Alexander Kaye, eds. 2014. *The Faith of Fallen Jews: Yosef Hayim Yerushalmi and the Writing of Jewish History*. Waltham, MA: Brandeis University Press.

Sackson, Adrian. 2015. Rationalistic Messianism and the Vicissitudes of History: The Final Chapter of Joseph Ibn Kaspi's *Tam ha-Kesef. Zutot: Perspectives on Jewish Culture* 12: 1–15.

Stewart, Matthew. 2014. *Nature's God: The Heretical Origins of the American Republic*. New York: Norton.

Yerushalmi, Yosef Hayim. 1982. *Zakhor: Jewish History and Jewish Memory*. Seattle, WA: University of Washington Press.

CHAPTER 3

America: Contexts and Cultures

From its beginnings, America regarded itself—and was regarded by others—as "different." America was a vast new territory that was oceans apart from other continents and cultures, and it emerged on the world stage centuries later than most western European and Far Eastern nations. Though it was inhabited for centuries by indigenous peoples with highly developed cultures of their own, America's newest arrivals from Europe seemingly had never encountered these peoples before in their wanderings throughout the globe. Compared to the crowded environs in Europe, America was a sparsely settled land with huge frontiers, diverse climates and topographies, and abundant natural resources.

Settlement of Europeans in America during the seventeenth century and beyond was rooted in the desire of various groups who were dissatisfied with continental society, economy, and government to carve out a new world. The United States of America ultimately was created by a confederation of diverse colonies that joined together in an experiment in democracy, liberty, and free enterprise. This newly founded entity had roots in European civilization, but over time created its own distinct culture of government, politics, language, arts, social structures, public institutions, and educational frameworks. America would become a retreat and a safe haven for millions of migrants from all over the world who sought refuge and a better life in this new world.

© The Author(s) 2017
B. Chazan et al., *Cultures and Contexts of Jewish Education*,
DOI 10.1007/978-3-319-51586-1_3

By the late nineteenth century, America had become an emergent player in world affairs, and by the twentieth century it came of age as a major force and factor in the dynamics of war and peace, commerce and industry, and all other aspects of international life. Throughout these eras, the "differentness" of America—in the way it promoted freedom, equality, and opportunity; its increasingly multicultural composition; and its young, inventive, and unrooted culture—was to define the nation's personality and appeal.

For Jews, America represented nothing less than a watershed in Jewish history. From the small but established Jewish presence in colonial times to the approximately seven million Jews of today, America's Jewish community has been incomparable. Most elements of modern Jewish life—among them the emergence of diverse orientations to Judaism; the tensions between individual freedom and the common good; the challenges of maintaining religious life in a mostly secular context; the affordances and constraints of organized Jewish communal activities, such as Jewish schooling; and the development of ethnic Jewish culture—originated or took shape on the American scene and in turn influenced modern Jewish communities the world over.[1] It is to the unique cultures and contexts of American Jewish life that we now turn our attention.

THE EVOLVING FOUNDATIONS OF AMERICAN JEWISH LIFE

Enlightenment thinking and its realization in the two great late-eighteenth-century revolutions (America and France) altered the societal structure within which Jews had lived for well over a millennium. As we have discussed, the corporate nature of pre-modern Western states had assigned secondary status to Jews and at the same time accorded them a semi-autonomous self-governing apparatus and a clearly delineated authority hierarchy, both of which were dismantled in the new modern societies. To move from secondary status to equality was a major boon for post-Emancipation Jews. However, the dismantling of the Jewish self-governing apparatus and the related authority hierarchy had negative implications for many aspects of Jewish communal living. As a result of these momentous changes, core Jewish beliefs and commitments underwent major modification.

The young American republic provided Jews a post-Emancipation context for Jewish life grounded in Enlightenment thinking. The United States emerged as a modern secular society that from its origins embraced the separation of church and state along with conceptions of individual citizenship, which applied to all members of society, religious identity not-withstanding. While the stimulus to this societal restructuring lay in the intense and bloody post-Reformation conflict among diverse Christian religious groupings, the new secular state was open to Jews and other non-Christians for their full participation and citizenship. What distinguished Jewish citizens from their fellow citizens was only their religious faith. In the process, Jewishness was transformed from an all-embracing ethnic and religious identity to a predominantly religious one.

Beginning in the middle decades of the seventeenth century, America had slowly accepted a small number of Jewish settlers (mostly Sephardic in origin), who had had lived for a period of time in Christian societies in which they were by and large involved in useful economic activities. The foundational group of Jews immigrating into the colonies created few problems for the colonial leadership, and this set a very positive foundation for subsequent Jewish life in America. When the colonies rebelled against the British king and established a new-style state based on Enlightenment principles, the small and well-integrated Jewish population raised no concerns with respect to extension of citizenship to them. The contentious debate over citizenship that had occurred in France and other places had no parallel in the United States.

Eventually Jewish immigration into America involved larger, more sequestered, and less westernized Jews. During the nineteenth century, more than 150,000 Jews from central Europe (mainly Germany, as well as Alsace, Galicia, Bohemia, Moravia, and Hungary) made their way to the United States. The foundations for Jewish citizenship had already been well established, and despite occasional outbursts of animosity toward the new German-Jewish immigrants, the possibility of denying citizenship to these Jews was never seriously considered. These German Jews found the environment of the young republic extremely congenial, and they quickly acculturated and prospered. By the time the largest wave of Jewish immigration to the United States arrived in the late nineteenth and early twentieth century, the prior German-Jewish immigrants were comfortably settled, had prospered economically, were well integrated into American life, and were fully prepared to extend helping hands to their new and somewhat problematic immigrating brethren.

The largest migration in Jewish history began at the outset of the 1880s and continued until the 1920s. By the end of this period of massive movement, more than two-and-a-half million Jews had made their difficult way across the Atlantic to settle in what they perceived to be a land of equality, security, and economic opportunity. This mass migration of Jews and others did provoke reservations and objections among groups of settled and established Americans. To be sure, the opposition was not uniquely directed at the Jewish immigrants, who constituted but one element in a larger southern and eastern European mass migratory movement; it was the overall migration—of which the Jews were but one component—that raised discomfort and opposition.

The eastern European Jewish immigrants had a number of factors in their favor in their adjustment to their new setting. These included the sturdy American foundations of equality for all, including Jews; the prior record of rapid Jewish acculturation to American life and culture; and the assistance of their successful and comfortably settled predecessors— who, concerned about both the wellbeing of their immigrant brethren and their own potentially endangered image in American society, offered considerable financial aid and social assistance to the Jewish newcomers. The support of the earlier Jewish immigrants was surely helpful; however, the rapid successes of the eastern European Jewish immigrants owed even more to the essential openness of American society, to the ambition and drive of the immigrants themselves, to the educational channels available for societal advancement, and to Jewish awareness and exploitation of these educational channels. While educational opportunity was prized and utilized by Jews in all post-Emancipation societies, the available educational channels were especially accessible in America and were exploited with special intensity in the twentieth-century United States.

Thus, the evolution of both America and of American Jewry created a solid foundation for Jewish life. America was heir to a rich legacy of Christian thinking, beginning in the Gospels and Paul and continued by many of the Church Fathers, which emphasized the virtues of the Jews, notwithstanding the negative Gospel imagery. This thinking lauded the Jews for constituting the very first human community to recognize the one true God and for serving as God's initial partner community for eons. Equally important, the Gospels and major Church thinkers pointed regularly to the undisputed reality that Jesus and his immediate followers were all themselves Jews. America was by no means immune to more negative medieval Christian images of the Jews or to the modern racially grounded anti-Semitism that sprang from alternative roots.[2] Nonetheless, negative imagery of and attitudes toward Jews in the United States never reached the depths and intensity or induced the harm that it did in Europe.

Ultimately, the balance of positive and negative attitudes toward Jews was dependent on the realities of non-Jewish and Jewish life in a given locale. Whereas in medieval Europe, the circumstances of Jewish life regularly tipped the scales in the negative direction, in America, when Jews were able to be seen as a useful and important social and economic factor, the hostility was minimized. The Jews of America were surely newcomers; however, they were not intruders in a well-established, homogeneous Christian society. America was different; Jews were newcomers in a society made up overwhelmingly of immigrants and their descendants.

Also, the economic specializations forced upon medieval and early modern European Jews were not part of the fabric of Jewish life in America. The openness of American society and the American economy allowed Jews far greater latitude in their vocational choices. Imagery of Jews as parasitic bankers and moneylenders surfaced from time to time, but it did not have anything like the traction it had in Europe, where the same imagery conjured up far more resonance and resentment. Overall, while America was hardly free of anti-Jewish sentiment, the level and impact of this anti-Jewish sentiment was considerably weaker than it was in Europe.

No less important is the fact that the culture of American society, with an openness to diverse religions, defined the Jews essentially as a religious group—different from Christians, for sure, but nonetheless categorically a religion. The separation of state and church was cardinal in American thought and practice; prior models of state and church were dismantled as part and parcel of the creation of this new nation. Because Jewishness had been redefined as religious identity, Jews, like other immigrants, were given essentially open latitude for integration in America.

However, as we have seen, the exclusive definition of Jewishness as religious identity was not the only option in modern society; ethnic, nationalist, socialist, and culturalist notions of Jewishness were also products of the Emancipation and Enlightenment. With respect to ethnic identity, America was once again quite different. It was obviously much newer as a national entity and culture, and thus lacked a fully formulated longstanding "American" ethnic identity. America was a country fashioned out of immigration, and the celebration of immigration—despite frequent opposition to new immigrants—became an essential element in American culture. Ellis Island and the Statue of Liberty welcomed all immigrants with an outstretched arm with the words of a Jewish poet, Emma Lazarus, saying, "Give me your tired, your poor. Your huddled masses yearning to breathe free." It was precisely this mix of nationalities and ethnicities that was widely depicted as a core and laudable feature of American culture and values. For most—although not all—Americans, maintenance of loyalty to places and cultures of origin was not at all antithetical to wholehearted American identity; rather, such loyalty was generally viewed as richly and genuinely American.

This openness to ethnic identification in America was a boon for Eastern European Jews raised in a Jewish culture that encompassed languages, mores, and folkways of an ancient people. Celebration of ethnic Jewish roots, Jewish ceremonies, traditional foods, Jewish language expressions, and Jewish humor was both thoroughly acceptable and totally in sync with the emergent multicultural America. For some American Jews, the religious option—either in traditional or altered forms—sufficed. For other American Jews, for whom religion was no longer compelling or even congenial, but who still had a desire to identify Jewishly, the options of ethnic or cultural identity were available. For still others, religious and cultural/national Jewish identity co-existed happily. For Jews of all types, America was "different," to be sure, for in contrast to the old country, it was above all hospitable.[3]

Lessons from the Immigrant Experience

The first engaging theme of early twentieth-century American Jewish culture was the immigrant experience itself.[4] The New York-based Jewish press served the diverse needs of new arrivals making their way in unfamiliar territory, presenting Jewish and general news; advertising jobs, local Jewish businesses, and communal organizations; offering help to locate relatives; and providing guidance on how to navigate their new lives. Multiple Jewish newspapers appeared daily, with either a religious, secular, socialist, or anarchist bent, and printed either in Yiddish, Ladino, or English. *Der Forverts* (*The Forward*), edited by Abraham Cahan, was the most prominent and long-lasting of the lot. *The Forward* printed daily news about New York, America, and the world, focusing especially on items of Jewish interest, along with original literature (e.g., the stories of the Yiddish writer Isaac Bashevis Singer) and the famous advice column, "A Bintel Brief."

The immigrant experience was also documented in Israel Zangwill's play, *The Melting Pot* (1908); Mary Antin's autobiography, *The Promised Land* (1912); Abraham Cahan's novel, *The Rise of David Levinsky* (1917); Anzia Yezierska's short stories, *Hungry Hearts* (1920); sociologist Louis Wirth's study, *The Ghetto* (1928); and Henry Roth's novel, *Call It Sleep* (1934). This literature focused on the challenges of dislocation and relocation, making a living, adjusting to new norms, and the conflict of the old and new, including generational strife.

The film *The Jazz Singer* (1927)—the first feature-length talking picture in America—recounted the archetypical saga of an immigrant Jew struggling between tradition and modernity. Jakie Rabinowitz (played originally by the Russian-born Jewish vaudeville veteran Al Jolson) is the musically talented son of the pious *hazan* (cantor) of a traditional Lower East Side synagogue.[5] Jakie breaks his father's heart by forsaking a career in the cantorate, changing his name to Jack Robin, and becoming a popular jazz and ragtime Hollywood and Broadway star who along the way divorces his faithful Jewish wife to marry the gentile dancer Mary Dale. Years later, Jack returns to New York to open in a new Broadway show on Yom Kippur eve, when he finds his father deathly ill and unable to lead the congregation in the hallowed *Kol Nidre* prayer. At the last moment, Jack forsakes his Broadway debut, puts on his father's cantorial garb, and leads the congregation in a soulful service. The film ends with various members of the Rabinowitz family joyously sitting in front row seats at the Broadway show while Jack performs on stage. In the end, *The Jazz Singer* celebrates the drive to escape the Old World while also acknowledging the dilemmas and ambivalence that come with embracing the New World.

The radio program *The Rise of the Goldbergs* (later the radio and television program *The Goldbergs*) likewise traced the rapid progression from the first difficult years of the immigrant experience to acceptance in the wider society. Molly Goldberg (played by Gertrude Berg) presented immigrant stories with an appropriate degree of authenticity and ethnicity, but also with an upbeat, positive, worldly view suitable for a broad American radio audience. The program, which aired in different versions from 1925 to 1966 (a revival of the television series aired in the 2010s), brought to light the saga of a typical immigrant family—coincidentally but recognizably Jewish—adjusting to America without abandoning their ethnic roots in a way that resonated with many other immigrant communities and made the Goldbergs' life a typical American story.

Expansive Jewish Opportunities in America

American Jews were delighted with the opportunities available to them in this different place with its unique worldview. Jews both felt the pressure and welcomed the opportunities to integrate fully into the surrounding society through economic activity, education, social relations, and political participation. The process of acculturation shaped Jewish communal activities as well. Community organization, synagogue rituals, religious ceremonies, spiritual beliefs, ethnic celebrations, social services, and schooling were all configured or reconfigured with an eye toward living comfortably as Jews within a broader secular, multicultural, pluralistic context.

Adjustment to the open American society epitomized American Jewish life in the twentieth century. Because the sequence of American Jewish history had never included an acrimonious debate over Jewish citizenship, American Jews did not feel the kinds of pressure perceived by their European Jewish brethren. The Jewish population in the United States underwent many of the same changes that were taking place in Europe—demographic, economic, educational, and cultural. However, the process of change in America was far less externally imposed and far less pressured. Rather, the changes that took place in American Jewry were much more internally generated in response to sociological developments, as well as in spontaneous and enthusiastic response to the new opportunities available in the open American ambience.

The eastern European Jews who made their way to the United States from the 1880s to the 1920s tended to settle initially in large immigrant neighborhoods in eastern seaboard cities. The most famous of these immigrant enclaves was the Lower East Side of New York City, owing to its massive population, but many eastern cities harbored similar neighborhoods. Ultimately, these venues would largely serve as way stations for a steady flow of newcomers who were likely to soon leave the teeming and squalid immigrant neighborhoods and settle in surroundings more salubrious for themselves and their families.

The geographic diffusion of Jews moved at a rapid pace and began to expand into nearby states and then throughout the country. As they became increasingly integrated and affluent, Jews opted for suburban areas, which resulted in yet further diminishment of the early tendency toward concentration in heavily Jewish enclaves. Out of all these developments came a new pattern of diffused Jewish habitation in American cities and indeed across the length and breadth of the United States. Once again, this development—like so much else on the post-Emancipation scene—was hugely beneficial to America's Jews as individuals, while weakening the hold of the Jewish community on its members.

Demographic diffusion was accompanied by economic diversification as well. America in the late nineteenth and early twentieth century was expanding rapidly in both its industrial and business sectors, and opportunities were plentiful and relatively open. Many of the immigrants found their initial niche as unskilled workers in the burgeoning clothing industry or as peddlers on the streets or out on the road, but they quickly moved beyond these points of economic entry. The immigrant Jews dreamed of and found independence through business, and many of them achieved the so-called American Dream. Businesses small and large were created by the immigrants, which resulted in numerous economic success stories. By the onset of World War II, many of these second-generation American Jews were well on their way to white-collar careers as teachers, pharmacists, and nurses, or even more ambitiously, as physicians or lawyers.

As depicted in such popular novels as Budd Schulberg's *What Makes Sammy Run?* (1941), Canadian writer Mordecai Richler's *The Apprenticeship of Duddy Kravitz* (1959), and Philip Roth's *Goodbye Columbus* (1959), the standard trajectory of second- and third-generation American Jews was out of the ethnic ghetto and into the wide world. To be sure, certain professional areas—like certain residential neighborhoods—were closed to Jews, but as a result of social and economic changes these barriers too began to fall.

During the intense war effort of World War II, many pre-existent social barriers were breached both in military and civilian settings. American Jewish males served fully in the US armed forces and derived the benefits that accrued from this military service and the enhanced social contacts with non-Jews that resulted. American Jewish women, like American women in general, were an important part of the civilian side of the war effort. Once again, this resulted in the post-war years in enhanced social contact and higher expectations of economic and social opportunity. Furthermore, in the wake of the war and not unrelated to the technological advances that played a role in American and Allied victory, new avenues of economic opportunity grounded in innovative technologies proliferated. These new economic sectors, like the burgeoning television and film industry and the exploding field of medical research, simply by virtue of their newness were open to Jews in a way that the older sectors of the economy were not. There was no entrenched leadership group that controlled these new sectors of the American economy. Jews thus made their way into the newly emergent economic sectors at every level, making maximal use of their opportunities.

Over the course of the twentieth century, America's Jews reveled in their increasing success and access to the upper echelons of American politics, business, culture, and society, represented by such leading figures as Louis D. Brandeis, Felix Frankfurter, Herbert Lehman, Jacob Schiff, Julius Rosenwald, Irving Berlin, Man Ray, Louis B. Mayer, Arthur Sulzberger, Albert Einstein, and later Joseph Lieberman, Ruth Bader Ginsburg, Ralph Lauren, Estée Lauder, Stephen Sondheim, Annie Leibovitz, Steven

Spielberg, Nora Ephron, Michael Bloomberg, Jonas Salk, and many more. (Another version of "making it" was through crime and other misdemeanors; thus, a lore grew up around the so-called Kosher Nostra, comprised of Jewish gangsters like Meyer Lansky, Bugsy Siegel, and Arnold Rothstein.) These trailblazers taught American Jews of all ages that Jews could become fully integrated into American life without necessarily abandoning their ethno-religious attachments. For many American Jews coming of age at mid-century, the ultimate symbol of "making it" was when, on October 6, 1965, the Brooklyn Dodgers' ace pitcher Sandy Koufax chose not to pitch in Game 1 of the World Series because it fell on Yom Kippur.

In the course of pursuing these economic changes and advances, Jews exploited the American public educational system perhaps more than any other ethnic group of the time. For Jews, as we shall see in the next chapter, public schooling was the gateway to full integration in America and into an emerging system of public higher education. Slowly, the number of admission slots open to Jews in America's elite private colleges and universities (previously limited by quotas) expanded as well, particularly as Jews' ability to pay full tuition and make philanthropic contributions to these institutions grew. Entrance into elite colleges paved the way for greater acceptance into highly regarded professional schools (medicine, law, business) and thus to even more lucrative careers for second- and third-generation American Jews. In addition, growing numbers of them began to consider academia as a career choice and prepared for the professoriate.

Among the most important developments in the education of America's Jews was the rise of academic Jewish studies on college and university campuses. The number of scholars of Jewish history, Bible, rabbinic texts, Jewish thought and philosophy, Jewish and Hebrew literature, Zionism and Israel, and the sociology of contemporary Jewry grew from a mere handful in the mid-twentieth century to well over 1000 in the early twenty-first century. Among their ranks were both Jews and non-Jews who, regardless of their own personal relationships with Judaism and Jewish life, were professionally committed to the rigorous and dispassionate scientific study of the Jewish experience for the purposes of strengthening general scholarship in these areas. Philanthropists sponsored chairs and departments of Jewish studies at almost every major private and public university in the United States and many liberal arts colleges as well. Scholars in these institutions produced a trove of books and articles published by major university presses, reviewed in scholarly journals, and debated at academic conferences.

In 1945, the American Jewish Committee created a monthly magazine called *Commentary* that focused on general political, sociological, and ideological issues, in addition to Jewish issues, and became one of the most important journals among the self-styled New York Intellectuals of mid-century. Many other new Jewish magazines (*Moment, Tikkun, Lilith*), blogs, and websites emerged over the years to serve as platforms for Jewish thought and discussion. A cadre of religious scholars and teachers, such as Mordecai Kaplan, Louis Finkelstein, Leo Jung, Norman Lamm, Joseph B. Soloveitchik, Alexander Schindler, and Rabbi Menachem Mendel Schneerson, and new age voices like Shlomo Carlebach, Zalman Schachter-Shalomi, Arthur Green, and Esther Jungreis, preached and taught at retreats, conferences, synagogues and through public media in an effort to vitalize Judaism among the increasingly secular American Jewish masses.

The three major rabbinical schools founded at the turn of the century—Hebrew Union College-Jewish Institute of Religion (Reform), The Jewish Theological Seminary (Conservative), and Yeshiva University (Orthodox)—were staffed by noteworthy scholars who trained generations of rabbis, cantors, and educators to serve the so-called Jews in the pews. Women's voices emerged increasingly in scholarship, poetry, and on religious matters, especially after Jewish feminist writers and leaders (Betty Friedan, Gloria Steinem, Bella Abzug, Letty Cottin Pogrebin) ascended the cultural and political stage in the 1960s, and the non-Orthodox seminaries began ordaining women rabbis in the 1970s and 1980s. The havurah movement, with its emphasis on living a vibrant Jewish life that is participatory and egalitarian (between men and women and between rabbis and lay people), emerged in the 1970s and was exemplified by the publication of the best-selling *The Jewish Catalog: A Do-It-Yourself Kit*. Books on Jewish studies, religion, culture, and civilization were published not only by the longstanding Jewish Publication Society, Schocken Books, Behrman House, and other Jewish presses, but also by many general trade publishers. A new genre of religious-themed Jewish fiction emerged as well, beginning with Milton Steinberg's *As a Driven Leaf* (1939) and continuing in more recent times with Anita Diamant's *The Red Tent* (1997), Maggie Anton's *Rashi's Daughters* (2007), and Dara Horn's *A Guide for the Perplexed* (2014). This literature is today accessible on e-readers and through smartphone apps. Indeed, there probably has been no other time when Jewish-themed books, texts, sources, and ideas have been as available and accessible as in contemporary America.

Organizing American Jewish Life

The unparalleled level of political, economic, social, and cultural acceptance and success for American Jewish individuals at the same time created serious problems for the efforts to fashion an effectively functioning and unified Jewish community. To the extent that Jews would organize themselves, it could only be voluntarily. Self-proclaimed Jewish leaders or small leadership cadres would have to convince a set of followers to join them in one or another important enterprise. If they were successful, voluntary organizations could be effectively created, although failure was by no means uncommon. Creating organizational structures for the American Jewish community began at the local level.

The most common manifestation of Jewish organizational life was the synagogue. Given the post-Emancipation definition of Jews as a religious grouping, the synagogue was the most ubiquitous Jewish organizational structure, and synagogues large and small were created all across the United States. At mid-century, American synagogues were the center of local Jewish life. They were architecturally modern, multipurpose structures with large sanctuaries, social halls, classrooms, libraries, playgrounds, and parking lots that neatly fit into the manicured environs of suburbia. American Jewry took special pride in places like the Beth Shalom Congregation in suburban Philadelphia designed by Frank Lloyd Wright, which was in Wright's words "a luminous Mt. Sinai" and which in 2007 was proclaimed a National Historic Landmark.[6]

Several generations of learned, knowledgeable, communicative rabbis led large, thriving congregations that typically provided Friday night, Saturday morning, and holiday services, Hebrew schools, youth groups, men's and women's clubs, and social service committees. Weekly synagogue newsletters chronicled marriages, *b'nei* and *b'not mitzvah*, holidays, memorials, and contributions, along with spiritual messages from the rabbi. Jewish learning for adults emerged in various forms, including lecture series, seminars, language workshops, retreats, and adult *b'nei* and *b'not mitzvah* classes. The synagogues were supported not only by regular dues-paying members and donors, but also from religious school fees (including early childhood programs through confirmation classes), space rental and catering for lifecycle events, and synagogue fundraisers.

The synagogue-as-church model fit neatly within the conformist, consensus, conservative post-World War II American milieu in which, as the sociologist Will Herberg posited in *Protestant-Catholic-Jew* (1955),

Jewishness was viewed as one of the three main religious categories in which Americans could be classified.[7] Herberg's analysis was remarkable insofar as Jews represented only a tiny portion of the American population, but it belied the outsized influence American Jews had in cultural industries such as journalism, film, academia, and the arts, as well as in business and political sectors. It suggested that Jews could be considered central players in the wider American society.

In 1946, a distinguished Boston-based congregational Reform rabbi, Joshua Loth Liebman, wrote *Peace of Mind*, part of a genre of pastoral self-help books that were aimed at mass audiences. It topped the *New York Times* bestseller list for more than a year. Not long after, Conservative theologian Abraham Joshua Heschel wrote *Man is Not Alone* (1951) and *God in Search of Man* (1955), focusing on the contemporary search for meaning. In the 1980s, Conservative rabbi Harold Kushner's *When Bad Things Happen to Good People* (1981) dealt with issues of theodicy, why people suffer, and how people can deal with evil and suffering in their lives. These books were generally regarded as popular Jewish theology, comparable to the writings of well-known liberal Christian theologians like Reinhold Niebuhr and Paul Tillich. The NBC radio and television program *The Eternal Light* (1944–1989), produced in conjunction with the Jewish Theological Seminary, was a popular weekly discussion of Jewish religious issues with larger spiritual and humanistic implications for a general American audience. This outreach work by knowledgeable Jews reflected the belief that Jewish tradition is not comprised only of prayer and ritual, but also encompasses moral ideas and actions relevant to dilemmas all Americans face.

The second half of the twentieth century also saw the emergence of the civil rights movement, in which American Jews played a significant role, as well as campaigns for the relief of Soviet Jewry and the mass resettlement of Iranian and Ethiopian Jews. Rallies, government lobbying, fundraising drives, social justice movements, and social service organizations made political activism a core of the American Jewish agenda. In these instances, American Jews learned Jewish history by making it.

THE HOLOCAUST IN AMERICAN JEWISH CULTURE

We have noted recurrently the differences between post-Emancipation developments in Europe and in the United States. These differences were highlighted in the experiences of the two sets of Jewries during the early to middle decades of the twentieth century. From the onset of the great immigration wave in the early 1880s, American Jews found increasing acceptance on the American scene, despite occasional outbursts of anti-Jewish sentiment. During this same period, however, antipathy to the Jews of Europe intensified markedly. In part, this intensification was stimulated by the introduction of a new theoretical framework for anti-Jewish thinking, rooted in developments in biology and anthropology, as well as weakened financial situations that convinced many Europeans—even highly educated Europeans—that Jews represented a profound threat to European civilization. Racist thinking provided clarity and ostensible legitimacy to anti-Jewish sentiment. To be sure, the wellsprings of much of the anti-Jewish sentiment lay in the traditional Christian negativity toward and fear of Judaism and Jews and in the longstanding European legacy of anti-Jewish attitudes. The fusion of the new racism and the older Christian and European anti-Jewish animus culminated in the explosive anti-Jewish sentiment that dominated the Nazi policies of the 1930s and 1940s, which began with exclusion of the Jews from much of organized German life in the 1930s and morphed into the policy of extermination that was articulated in the early 1940s and carried out thereafter.

By the end of World War II, much of Europe lay in ruins, millions had been killed during the fighting, and the bulk of European Jewry had been destroyed in a carefully planned and executed program of genocide. The great centers of European Jewish life no longer existed, and the still young Jewish community of the United States had become the colossus of the post-war Jewish world, bearing heightened responsibilities and experiencing new sensitivities. Post-war American Jewish life, American Jewish identity, and American Jewish education were deeply affected consciously and unconsciously by the horrors of the Holocaust, which became a prominent fixture in American Jewish culture in subsequent decades.

The Diary of Anne Frank (1952), Elie Wiesel's *Night* (1956), and Primo Levi's *Survival in Auschwitz* (1959); Raul Hilberg's *The Destruction of the European Jews* (1961), Hannah Arendt's *Eichmann in Jerusalem* (1963), and Lucy Dawidowicz's *The War Against the Jews* (1975); and Stanley Kramer's star-studded *Judgement at Nuremberg* (1961), Claude Lanzmann's epic *Shoah* (1985), the four-part NBC television mini-series *The Holocaust* (1978), and Steven Spielberg's Academy Award-winning *Schindler's List* (1993) joined a raft of personal memoirs, scholarly studies, and documentary and feature films about the Holocaust produced in the 1950s–1990s that gained widespread attention and acclaim. In 1978, President Jimmy Carter created the President's Commission on the Holocaust, chaired by Elie Wiesel, which in 1993 opened the United States Holocaust Memorial Museum on Raoul Wallenberg Place, adjacent to the National Mall in Washington, DC. In 1996, Professor Deborah Lipstadt, a renowned Holocaust scholar at Emory University, was charged in a British court with libel for characterizing the writer David Irving's infamous work as Holocaust denial. The four-year trial on the veracity of Holocaust historiography, in which Lipstadt ultimately prevailed, was a courtroom saga compelling enough to inspire a major Hollywood feature film, *Denial* (2016).

Throughout the latter part of the twentieth century, the slogan "Never Again!" and the attendant imperative to commemorate and study the Holocaust became de rigueur in Jewish schools, synagogues, community centers, youth groups, and heritage tours. Teaching the Holocaust was also mandated in the public schools of five states (California, Florida, Illinois, New Jersey, New York) and included in the social studies curriculum standards of most other states.

AMERICAN JEWS AND ISRAEL

At the same time that European racism against Jews was on the rise in the late nineteenth century, Jews of eastern and central European roots were beginning to advance the agenda of Jewishness as national identity. Like many of their neighbors, these Jews sought to realize their national identity through creation of a nation-state that would embody and express their national legacy and yearnings. Precisely what kind of state and where that state might be located were matters of considerable contention among the eastern European Jewish national movements, but with the passage of time the group that was committed to creating the Jewish state in the historical homeland of the Jewish people—the Land of Israel—materialized as the dominant nationalist movement on the Jewish scene.

The effort to create a Jewish state in Palestine emerged in American Jewish consciousness in the early decades of the twentieth century partly due to the leadership of Supreme Court Justice Louis D. Brandeis, who saw Zionism and Americanism as fundamentally compatible through their mutual commitments to democracy and social justice. In May 1942, just as the Final Solution intensified in Europe, 600 leaders from across North America and 18 world countries attended an emergency conference at the Biltmore Hotel in New York and created what became known as the "Biltmore Program," affirming the creation of a Jewish homeland in

Palestine and the immigration of millions of Jews as the agenda of world Jewry. The parallel emergence of the Holocaust in Europe and increasing Jewish advocacy in America for a Jewish nation-state were to have profound personal and communal implications for American Jews.

For many American Jews, it was their brothers and sisters who were being exterminated by the Nazis, and for others it was their brothers and sisters who had chosen to move to the growing Jewish settlements in Palestine. American Jewry was intimately linked to these historic events, supportive of the efforts of Palestinian Jewry, and devastated by the fate of European Jewry. A sense of Jewish communal responsibility was felt with special force by American Jewry, which was now viewed—and indeed viewed itself—as the largest and most influential Jewish community in the world. While many sectors of American Jewry had previously been lukewarm at best regarding the Zionist project, the post-World War II awareness of American Jewry's new role on the world scene, the needs of the young state, and the importance of Israel for the salvation of the remnant of European Jewry combined to elevate Israel to a primary concern of American Jewry.

David Ben-Gurion, Golda Meir, and other Zionist leaders made numerous visits to the United States to speak to small and large gatherings, endearing themselves and their cause among American Jews. Articles about Palestine, immigration, and the efforts for statehood appeared in large circulation newsletters such as *National Jewish Monthly* (B'nai B'rith) and the *Hadassah Magazine* (Hadassah). Major newspapers like the *New York Times*, *New York Post*, and *Daily News* reported regularly on events in Palestine and Israel. American Jews also learned about the growing Jewish presence in Israel through photographs and films, books, poems, memoirs, and children's stories, as well as lessons in modern Hebrew, Israeli folk dancing, and perhaps most ubiquitously, blue metal *pushkes* (charity boxes) that appeared in synagogues, schools, and homes nationwide in support of the Jewish National Fund. The United Nations roll call vote conferring recognition of Israel's statehood in 1947 was heard live on radios in Jewish living rooms throughout the United States. American Jews felt enormous pride in the accomplishments of the new Jewish state.

The State of Israel rose to prominence in American popular culture with the publication of Leon Uris' book *Exodus* (1958) and the release of Otto Preminger's film version starring Paul Newman (1960). *Exodus* and other like feature films (e.g., *Cast a Giant Shadow* (1966) with Kirk Douglas and *Judith* (1966) with Sophia Loren) created an epic narrative about Israel's heroic origins that survived for decades, influencing Jews and non-Jews in America and abroad. The narrative featured a new, strong, bold Jewish persona committed to creating a Jewish homeland and political state that would be rooted in Western values, linked to Jewish history, and safe for millions of Jews in need. Israel's pioneers, according to this narrative, faced a constant barrage of ambushes, terrorist raids, and warfare with hostile neighbors and non-Jewish indigenous populations, but persevered with passion, power, and conviction. The founding of Israel, in the eyes of the intrepid pioneers and their international supporters, was about turning ancient cities and desert frontiers into a prosperous modern nation that would become the only Western democracy in the Middle East.

The months leading up to and immediately following the Six-Day War in 1967 were a time of great tension and then overflowing joy among American and world Jewry, as Israel proved its ability to survive an existential threat efficiently and in fact mightily. This historical moment also marked the beginning of over 50 years of very complicated political dynamics inside and outside Israel that included the challenges and travails of the Yom Kippur War (1973), the United Nations' "Zionism is Racism" resolution (1975), peace treaties with Egypt (1979) and Jordan (1994), the Lebanon War (1982), recurrent Palestinian intifadas (1987–1993, 2000–2005), the mass proliferation of Jewish settlements in the West Bank and Gaza Strip, and the assassination of Prime Minister Yitzhak Rabin by an Israeli Jew (1995). Meanwhile, Israel also emerged as a military powerhouse and economic dynamo—a so-called start-up nation—with astounding achievements in such areas as high tech, medicine, and communications.[8] These various historical circumstances were accompanied in the United States by a dramatic expansion of forceful Israel advocacy by organizations such as the American Israel Public Affairs Committee (AIPAC) and the rise of vociferous progressive pro-Israel movements such as Peace Now and J Street, which together reflected American Jewish engagement with, including critiques of, Israel.

Over the decades, contemporary life in Israel was introduced into popular American and American Jewish culture by the translation into English of the works of significant Israeli literary figures such as Amos Oz, A.B. Yehoshua, David Grossman, Yehuda Amichai, and Etgar Keret, who described the complex inner dynamics and personalities of the modern Jewish state; by the growth of Jewish film festivals that brought Israeli first-run feature films to American audiences (e.g., *Sallah* (1964), *Operation Thunderbolt* (1977), *Waltz with Bashir* (2008), *Footnote* (2011)); by remakes of popular Israeli television shows for American audiences (*In Treatment* (2008–2010) and *Homeland* (2011–2017)); by the increasing popularity of Israeli cuisine among American cooks and foodies (e.g., Yotam Ottolenghi's cookbooks,

Michael Solomonov's and Einat Admony's restaurants); and by the massive growth of educational tourism in Israel (e.g., Taglit-Birthright, gap year yeshiva programs, synagogue missions, teen tours).

In the twenty-first century, technology has enabled Israel's day-to-day life to be experienced by Jews worldwide in real time, whether by videoconferencing with family and friends, receiving missile warnings and all-clear signals over smart phones, or just watching Israeli music videos online. Israel is no longer a far off wonderland or never-never land for American Jewry; rather, it is immediate and real, with all its scars and smiles, warts and wonder.

SECULAR AMERICAN JEWISH CULTURE

A vibrant secular culture grew out of the minds and hands of second- and third-generation American Jews who no longer dealt with themes of strangeness and belonging, but rather adjustment and complacency. Perhaps the most important exemplars of this culture was a group of writers—Saul Bellow, Philip Roth, and Bernard Malamud—whose personal life histories and many of their characters and stories dealt with Jewish contexts, although they did not regard themselves as "Jewish authors" per se. They and others such as Grace Paley, Joseph Heller, Marge Piercy, Howard Nemerov, Muriel Rukeyser, and Adrienne Rich, as well as playwrights such as Arthur Miller, Neil Simon, David Mamet, and Wendy Wasserstein, created a remarkable literature recognized with National Book Awards, Pulitzer Prizes, and Nobel Prizes.

Some of these writers referred to their childhood Jewish neighborhoods (Roth's Newark, Piercy's Detroit, Simon's New York), but these were not immigrant stories or literature; rather, their topics were alienation, identity, morality, dysfunction, sexuality, self-fulfillment, angst, humor, and liberation. The cinema counterpart to these authors was Woody Allen, many of whose films (*Annie Hall* (1977), *Manhattan* (1979), *Zelig* (1983), *Radio Days* (1987), *Crime and Misdemeanors* (1989)) included Jewish venues, foods, accents, words, and memories, but mainly centered on common dilemmas of anxiety, meaning, meaninglessness, jazz, and death. The television counterpart was Larry David, whose immensely popular sitcoms *Seinfeld* (1989-1998) and *Curb Your Enthusiasm* (2000-2011, 2017) sometimes dabbled in Jewish themes but always evoked classic Jewish humor and sensibilities, much to the appreciation of general audiences.

A twenty-first-century generation of writers who incorporate Jewish themes, such as Rebecca Goldstein, Nathan Englander, Gary Shteyngart,

Jonathan Safran Foer, Boris Fishman, Nicole Krauss, and Michael Chabon, are more knowledgeable and comfortable with their roots in Jewish life and culture and deal more fluidly with the Jewish and the general than many of their predecessors. These authors are neither self-conscious with respect to nor disconnected from their Jewishness; their work reflects a more nuanced and reflective interaction of Jewish themes with perennial issues of marriage, divorce, childrearing, terror, meaning-making, and other characteristics of the postmodern condition.

There have been Jewish voices in the music world as well. Some of America's most popular songs, compositions, and musicals were penned by Jews, among them Irving Berlin ("God Bless America," "White Christmas"), Aaron Copland ("Fanfare for the Common Man"), George Gershwin (*Rhapsody in Blue*), Richard Rodgers (*The Sound of Music*), Leonard Bernstein (*West Side Story*), Sheldon Harnick and Jerry Bock (*Fiddler on the Roof*), and Jonathan Larson (*Rent*). Robert Zimmerman, born in 1941 to a middle-class Jewish family in Hibbing, Minnesota, at a certain point reinvented himself as Bob Dylan and linked his history to riding the American rails in the folk tradition of Woody Guthrie. While there are Dylan scholars who seek and find Jewish motifs, themes, and characters in his songs and life, he is clearly an American troubadour, creator, and innovator above all. Much the same can be said of other 1950s–2000s popular musicians like Paul Simon and Art Garfunkel, Carole King, Burt Bacharach, Barry Manilow, Carly Simon, Billy Joel, Gene Simmons and Paul Stanley (KISS), Lou Reed, The Ramones, David Lee Roth, Paula Abdul, Lenny Kravitz, Beck, Mike Gordon and Jon Fishman (Phish), and Adam Levine, whose Jewish roots have been imperceptible in their creative work, let alone their personal lives, but who nonetheless have been recognized by their ethnically prideful American Jewish fans as Jewish musicians.

Few celebrities embraced the mantle of "American Jewish artist" like Barbra Streisand, whose career was rooted in ballads, songs, and films that dealt with general themes of love, loss, people, beauty, and sadness, but who also was comfortable playing a traditional Jewish woman in *Yentl* (1983) and a classic "Jewish mother" in *Meet the Fockers* (2004), as well as singing "Hatikvah" to Israeli Prime Minister Golda Meir at a ceremony honoring Israel's 30th anniversary and "Avinu Malkeynu" in Jerusalem at Israeli President Shimon Peres' 90th birthday party. Streisand, who reportedly was derided in her childhood and early career for looking and acting "too Jewish," famously refused to surgically alter her prominent nose or lose her Brooklyn Jewish accent. She did not need to do so in order to be an American superstar.[9]

COMMUNAL COHESION AND ITS DIFFICULTIES

Jews on the individual level benefitted dramatically from the opportunities offered by the expanding openness of American society. At the same time, the blessings of demographic diffusion, economic diversification, and social mixing weakened the cohesion of the American Jewish community. Those committed to maintaining Jewish communal life encountered great difficulties in organizing their fellow Jews effectively and had to search for new ways to bring together diverse sets of Jews no longer congregated in identifiably Jewish neighborhoods, professions, and social clusters.

The lack of government support of religious institutions in modernity and in America in particular meant that there was no leadership group that could declare one or another form of synagogue worship or ritual behavior legitimate or illegitimate. Alongside the diversity of synagogues that had been founded by immigrants from different regions and cultures (e.g., Ashkenazic and Sephardic) throughout the globe, denominationalism emerged, and synagogues were increasingly affiliated with one of them. All three major Jewish denominations—Orthodox, Conservative, and Reform—established national organizational structures that included rabbinical seminaries, rabbinical organizations, and lay organizations. Led by figures of note, all three organizational structures provided cohesion, resources, and a sense of corporate identity to these denominations.

This overarching diversity among the movements regarding religious doctrine and praxis was accompanied by the essentially local nature of the individual synagogue. Not only did denominations differ from each other, but local synagogues in the same denomination also often differed in outlook and practice, sometimes considerably. To an extent, the differences were geographic; synagogues of any of the three major denominations in the Northeast were quite different from congregations of the same denomination in the Midwest or the Far West, depending on the extent to which shifts in the central denominational organizations, based in New York City, made their way to farther reaches of the country, as well as the extent to which regional cultures differed from national normative models. On the most local level, the tone of particular synagogues was set by its founders or by influential rabbis; this tone then determined the makeup and character of the congregations.

While synagogues were the most common form of voluntary Jewish organizational life, the legacy of pre-modern Jewish institutions combined with the needs of the immigrant community resulted in new organizational structures in America. Prominent among these structures were those oriented toward assistance for Jews in need. Given the poverty from which many of the eastern European immigrants fled and the lack of economic skills with which they reached America, the needs were often extreme. Once again, the previously settled Jews were prepared to offer aid, to an extent out of genuine sympathy and to an extent in order to obviate negative imagery of impoverished Jews as a burden on America. At the same time, the immigrants themselves—long used to the Jewish community structure with its network of social services—quickly reproduced some of these agencies in their new and radically different setting. Jews proved quite effective in caring for their own.

As was typical of the American context, diversification was the rule. Multiple local organizations oriented toward assisting needy Jews sprang up, grounded in common points of European origin or in shared philanthropic concerns. In pre-modern Jewish communities, effective negotiation with the non-Jewish world—which meant the non-Jewish authorities of church and state—had been a crucial communal responsibility, generally carried out by a small and well-placed set of religious and wealthy communal leaders. This kind of advocacy was maintained in America, but was modified in the context of the absence of any formal relationship between the government and religious groups and of the new and democratic tenor of American life. Various Jewish groups emerged to look out for the rights and needs of American Jews, leading to the creation of a network of Jewish defense and advocacy organizations—Anti-Defamation League, American Jewish Committee, American Jewish Congress—oriented toward protecting the image of Jews and Judaism and the experience of American Jews.

While some of this effort was directed at governmental bodies and figures, the democratic thrust of American life translated into a broader effort to influence popular opinion and to create for the American public at large more positive imagery of Judaism, Jews, and especially Jewish immigrants. American Jewry became the locus of a rich panoply of organizations, competing for limited resources and pursuing alternative objectives. All these orientations—to religious life and practice, assistance to Jews in need, and defense of Jewish interests and the Jewish image—involved the establishment of discrete and focused institutions led by increasingly charismatic and skilled professionals who were to assume the mantle of leaders of the Jewish community.

Paralleling large-scale communal organization was an effort at organization on the local level, beyond the synagogue that was ostensibly tailored to meet spiritual, religious, and lifecycle needs. For the purposes of more effectively raising charitable funds and distributing these funds more rationally, many Jewish communities established local "federations" of local service organizations oriented primarily toward philanthropy. All across the United States, Jewish communities fashioned for themselves these central agencies for the modest purpose of raising and disbursing philanthropic funds. The federations came to represent the most successful effort at bringing together the diverse strands of American Jewry at the local level.

At the same time, fragmentation was also a major feature of twentieth-century-Jewish life in the United States. Precisely the latitude that America offered for Jewish identification—which we have noted as a boon for American Jewry—had its disadvantages as well. One of the prices of free entry into the wider society was a noticeable rise in assimilation and inter-marriage rates among rank-and-file American Jews. Sociological studies through the latter part of the twentieth century, culminating in the momentous 1990 National Jewish Population Study, showed that more than 50% of young Jews were marrying non-Jews, many of them were forsaking religious life, and many ultimately were not raising their children Jewish.[10]

Federations and national communal organizations were united in alarm over the situation but developed increasingly disparate and sometimes contentious proposals and programs for dealing with the perceived crisis. In fact, in the 1980s and 1990s American Jewish scholars and communal leaders were more likely to raise questions such as "Will there be one Jewish people by the year 2000?" (the subject of a 1986 conference organized by CLAL, the National Jewish Center for Learning and Leadership) and "Religious Movements in Collision: A Jewish Culture War?" (the title of a chapter in historian Jack Wertheimer's 1994 book, *A People Divided: Judaism in Contemporary America*) than they were able to point up truly effective efforts at unified action and organization among American Jews. Jews had become so integrated into American society that the Jewish community became as differentiated internally as the multicultural society surrounding it.

BEING JEWISH IN AMERICA

We now see a wide diversity in ideas about and experiences of Jews, Jewishness, and Judaism in contemporary American culture—an outgrowth of the consilience between the agenda of the twentieth- and twenty-first-century American Jewish community and the broader American society on such issues as integration into America; the values of liberty, rights, and democracy; and religion as a desirable private choice. Less resolved is the question of what constitutes Jewishness to begin with. Is it belief? Prayer? Ritual? Synagogue membership? Holidays? Lifecycle events? Heredity? Heritage? The Lower East Side? Israel? The Holocaust? Jewish guilt? Jewish humor? Bagels and lox? Jewish arts? All of these, some of them, or none?

Some communal policymakers, stakeholders, and scholars are deeply concerned with pursuing the answer. American Jews have long been at home in America; American Jewish political, economic, and cultural trail-blazers demonstrate that a Jew can be almost anything in America and that Jews are like all other people and peoples. Then again, there are moments, traditions, heritages, memories, and other vestiges of Jewish life that do not fade. Ultimately, American Jews are free to live Jewishly or not, but for those committed to the endurance of the Jewish community the question of how to ensure that it endures is a pressing one.

A quintessential response to the quandary of Jewish survival in the open American context has been the creation and evolution of a new system of American Jewish education for the new American Jewish community. The contexts, contours, and culture of American Jewish schooling are the subject we turn to next.

NOTES

1. The two most prominent scholarly surveys of American Jewish history are Hasia R. Diner, *The Jews of the United States, 1654–2000* (Berkeley: University of California Press, 2006), and Jonathan Sarna, *American Judaism: A History* (New Haven, CT: Yale University Press, 2005).
2. On the more and less positive Christian imageries of Judaism and Jews, see Robert Chazan, *From Anti-Judaism to Anti-Semitism* (Cambridge: Cambridge University Press, 2016).
3. For a fascinating discussion of the relationship between European and American Jewish history, see Christian Wiese and Cornelia Wilhelm, eds., *American Jewry: Transcending the European Experience?* (London: Bloomsbury Publishing, 2016).
4. See Stephen J. Whitfield, "Declarations of Independence: American Jewish Culture in the Twentieth Century," in *Cultures of the Jews: A New History*, ed. David Biale (New York: Schocken Books, 2002).
5. *The Jazz Singer* was remade in 1952 with Danny Thomas, in 1959 with Jerry Lewis, and in 1980 with Neil Diamond.

6. Blair Kamin, "Structure blends spirituality and sustainability: Designers aim for greenest synagogue in America," *Chicago Tribune*, February17, 2008, http://articles.chicagotribune.com/2008-02-17/news/0802150519_1_ jewish-architecture-jewish-studies-beth-shalom-synagogue
7. Will Herberg, *Protestant-Catholic-Jew: An Essay in American Religious Sociology* (Garden City, NY: Doubleday, 1955).
8. Dan Senor and Saul Singer, *Start-Up Nation: The Story of Israel's Economic Miracle* (New York: Twelve, 2009).
9. Neal Gabler, *Barbra Streisand: Redefining Beauty, Femininity, and Power* (New Haven, CT: Yale University Press, 2016).
10. Barry A. Kosmin and others, *Highlights of the CJF 1990 National Jewish Population Study* (New York: The Council of Jewish Federations, 1991), 14.

BIBLIOGRAPHY

Chazan, Robert. 2016. *From Anti-Judaism to Anti-Semitism*. Cambridge: Cambridge University Press.
Diner, Hasia R. 2006. *The Jews of the United States, 1654–2000*. Berkeley: University of California Press.
Gabler, Neal. 2016. *Barbra Streisand: Redefining Beauty, Femininity, and Power*. New Haven, CT: Yale University Press.
Herberg, Will. 1955. *Protestant-Catholic-Jew: An Essay in American Religious Sociology*. Garden City, NY: Doubleday.
Kamin, Blair. 2008. Structure Blends Spirituality and Sustainability: Designers Aim for Greenest Synagogue in America. *Chicago Tribune*, February 17. http://articles.chicagotribune.com/2008-02-17/news/0802150519_1_ jewish-architecture-jewish-studies-beth-shalom-synagogue
Kosmin, Barry A., and Others. 1991. *Highlights of the CJF 1990 National Jewish Population Study*. New York: The Council of Jewish Federations.
Sarna, Jonathan. 2005. *American Judaism: A History*. New Haven, CT: Yale University Press.
Senor, Dan, and Saul Singer. 2009. *Start-Up Nation: The Story of Israel's Economic Miracle*. New York: Twelve.
Whitfield, Stephen J. 2002. Declarations of Independence: American Jewish Culture in the Twentieth Century. In *Cultures of the Jews: A New History*, ed. David Biale. New York: Schocken Books.
Wiese, Christian, and Cornelia Wilhelm, eds. 2016. *American Jewry: Transcending the European Experience?* London: Bloomsbury Publishing.

CHAPTER 4

The Culture of American Jewish Schooling

American Jewry's dynamic, complex, and sometimes paradoxical effort to balance the prerogatives of American citizenship with the responsibilities of Jewish distinctiveness found its ultimate expression in the twentieth-century education of American Jewish youth. On one hand, the majority of new American Jews were preoccupied with full integration into American society, and the free public school system was a primary means to that end. On the other hand, many Jewish immigrants brought with them memories of powerful Jewish educational formats from the Old World, including traditional *heders* (one-room schoolhouses), *talmud torahs* (community-sponsored schools), *yeshivas* (all-day schools), and secular Bundist (socialist) schools, and they sought to revitalize these structures in the New World.

According to the popular understanding of the Jewish immigrant experience at the turn of the twentieth century, Jewish schooling lost the battle with public schooling early on:

Predisposed to schooling upon arrival, encouraged and assisted to enroll in public school by the established Jewish community and the service institutions it had created, unable initially to organize and finance schools of their own, compelled by law to send their children, boys *and* girls, to school where they could best be transformed into good, law-abiding Americans who could speak and comport themselves in the "proper" American manner,

© The Author(s) 2017
B. Chazan et al., *Cultures and Contexts of Jewish Education*,
DOI 10.1007/978-3-319-51586-1_4

and last, but not least, the children's desire to be like other children, to be knowledgeable and participating members of *their* native American culture, it is no wonder that immigrant children flocked to New York's public schools… and away from more traditional forms of Jewish education…[1]

It is estimated that more than 90% of immigrant Jews living in New York City in the early part of the century attended public schools, and Jewish children made up nearly 40% of the total elementary school population in the city.[2]

At the same time, in that era, 25 percent or more of elementary-aged Jewish students attending public schools also attended supplementary Jewish schools, which met on weekday afternoons and/or Sunday mornings. Jewish supplementary schooling was intended to counteract the potential estrangement of Jewish youth from their native ethno-religious community by providing a concrete, institutionalized, traditional connection to Jewish life. And while many immigrant Jews were willing to sacrifice elements of Jewish tradition and observance for the sake of entrance into the American mainstream, others saw the prospect of living comfortably in two worlds—American and Jewish—at once. For this reason, they sought to build up a system of Jewish schooling that could complement public schooling, together producing the quintessential "American Jew."

The emergent American Jewish supplementary school system ultimately encompassed thousands of institutions, millions of students and educators, and billions of dollars in annual expenditures.[3] Once the full-fledged supplementary school system was in place, by the middle of the twentieth century, it became the dominant framework for American Jewish education that—with some modifications—still remains in place.

Our interest in this chapter is how and why Jewish schooling became the most legitimated—by which we mean, the most commonly accepted and practiced—form of Jewish education on the American scene. From *heders* to Sunday schools to afternoon Hebrew schools to day schools, Jewish schooling became permanently etched in the collective memory and ethos of American Jewry. To this day, most adult American Jews either enthusiastically support Jewish schooling or stridently reject it, but few of them have no opinion on the subject: such is its impact on the fabric of American Jewry. More pointedly, supplementary Jewish schools often have been the scourge of Jewish children, the scapegoat of Jewish policymakers, the thorn in Jewish parents' sides, and the butt of Jewish jokes, and yet the overwhelming majority of American Jews have attended them for at least one year. The sociologist David Schoem claims that, for American Jewry, supplementary Jewish schooling is essentially a ritual act of Jewish connection and commitment. In his ethnography of a Jewish afternoon school, Schoem quotes one exasperated Jewish parent who confesses:

> On occasion Eddie has told us that he hates Hebrew school. I say, "Edward, that's wonderful. You're carrying on a Jewish tradition. Because when I went to Hebrew school, I hated it, too. Because all good Jews hate Hebrew school."[4]

Indeed, supplementary Jewish schooling is a powerful cultural touchstone among American Jews. Our focus is on the structures and ideals at the heart of this culture.

EDUCATION, SCHOOLING, AND THE CULTURE OF SCHOOLING

Before proceeding, a few key definitions are in order. "Education," in the popular imagination, usually involves a place called school, but in fact the process of education encompasses a much broader complex of experience, learning, and growth. With historian Lawrence Cremin, we understand education as "the deliberate, systematic, and sustained effort to transmit, evoke, or acquire knowledge, values, attitudes, skills, or sensibilities, as well as any learning that results from the effort, direct or indirect, intended or unintended."[5] Such a broad-based definition is intended to imply that education happens purposefully or coincidentally in a wide range of institutions and entities—in addition to schools—that also impart knowledge, transmit culture, and shape social behavior, such as families, social networks, houses of worship, libraries, museums, computers, media outlets, workplaces, and summer camps. Jewish learning over the ages took place at home, in the synagogue, in schools, and in the community, and it happened in interactions between children and parents, students and teachers, disciples and rabbis, and in the realm of self-education. Jewish education happens nowadays in a wide range of meaningful settings as well, aside from schools.

In America, however, "schooling" historically has been the primary means by which the society educates its young. The very purpose of state-sponsored schooling was to protect rights, maintain law and order, promote productivity, and, most important, cultivate good character, for (it was believed) only a civic-minded, industrious, and moral citizenry could properly participate in the new representative form of government and free market economy. Thus, for the sake of maintaining democracy and striving toward meritocracy, the American people put their stock in schools and colleges. The school's function *in loco parentis* both reflected and shaped the evolving American belief that the school—rather than parents—had the primary responsibility to shape the young to be "American," literate, well-trained, and work- and college-ready.

By the twentieth century, farm, factory, and artisan apprenticeships for children and adolescents gave way to compulsory schooling. Meantime, schooling increasingly shifted from denominational, religiously based grammar schools and seminaries to public elementary schools and comprehensive high schools. In due course, the American Dream became associated with schooling, as graduating high school became a minimum desideratum and attaining a college degree an ultimate achievement. Public schools came to be the most familiar of all of America's civic institutions, and schooling became embedded in the daily lives of children, families, and neighborhoods. The ever-present armies of yellow school busses and school crossing guards have come to be a daily reminder of the centrality of school in American life.

It is estimated that, on any given day, close to one-quarter of America's population, comprised of children, teachers, and staff, inhabits school buildings.[6] The school curriculum—its subject areas, core contents, textbooks, pedagogical methods, values, structures, power dynamics, and intended outcomes, all of which historians David Tyack and Larry Cuban refer to as the "grammar of schooling"—became a *lingua franca* among American children.[7] Schooling extended to evenings and weekends as well, in after-school extracurricular activities such as sports, theater, newspaper, and school dances, as well as in in parochial religious, language, or ethnic supplementary schools. In these and other ways, schools became ubiquitous in American culture, and education in America became synonymous with schooling.

When we say that a distinctive "culture of American Jewish schooling" evolved over time, we mean that (1) Jewish schooling became an essential element of American Jewish culture and a rite of passage in which most American Jews participate in one way or another at some point in their lives, and (2) Jewish schooling is itself an American Jewish cultural artifact that embodies a set of social, political, and intellectual mores, traditions, customs, and beliefs about how the ideal young member of the American Jewish community should think, feel, and act. In both these senses, Jewish schooling signifies an American Jewish *paideia*, that is, a culture that has always affirmed the centrality of public education along with some form of Jewish schooling to the community. What form this schooling should take is another story, to which we now turn our attention.

AMERICAN JEWRY'S "LOVE AFFAIR" WITH PUBLIC SCHOOLS

Since the early days of the republic, America's public schools were intended, in large part, to prepare future citizens for active and effective participation in democratic society. In the name of national unity, homogenization of the student body was the rule, and nonconformity was assiduously avoided. Most common school advocates believed that public education, common to all people (at least hypothetically), could serve as society's great equalizer. By promoting Anglo-Saxon, Protestant, middle class, democratic, "American" values, the schools would ultimately create a harmonious body politic comprised of "good Americans."[8]

The influx of over twenty million immigrants to the United States in the late nineteenth and early twentieth centuries caused civic leaders and public school administrators to reassess their goals, particularly in rapidly industrializing urban areas where newcomers settled in large concentrations. Progressive Era reformers called upon established civic institutions, including settlement houses, welfare organizations, and especially public schools, to teach the "uncivilized" newcomers more "respectable" forms of culture, manners, and morals.[9] The greatest focus was placed on the immigrants' children, who presumably could be molded into "good Americans" from an early age. Educators and social workers began defining their roles *in loco parentis* more extensively, based on the assumption that Old World parents were unwilling to or incapable of getting their children to adjust to American life, and state institutions were in any case more suited to instilling public mores. Compulsory school attendance laws were passed in order to move immigrant youths off the streets and out of the workplace and into Americanization and vocational programs. New schoolhouses were built, centralized authority systems were developed, and massive bureaucracies were put in place so that the explosion in public school enrollment and activities could be administered efficiently. Curriculum offerings were streamlined accordingly; for example, high school students were funneled into differentiated academic and vocational tracks based on the students' proven learning abilities and their predicted occupational roles.[10]

With respect to immigrants in particular, some educational reformers pushed for a powerful, rapid, and thoroughgoing form of assimilation through heavy-handed lessons in English language and American history, government, civics, patriotism, heroes, and holidays, all of which they hoped would eradicate any ties immigrants had to their ancestral cultures, languages, and values. "It becomes more urgent with every new and alien source of emigration to the United States that is opened, and almost with every new shipload of arriving immigrants," wrote the *New York Times* in an 1894 editorial. "The more remote and alien from our language, institutions, and ways of thinking the new-comers are, the greater is the necessity that their children shall receive our public education."[11] Other educators took a more gradual approach to acculturation by promoting "American" moral values such as industry, benevolence, temperance, and cleanliness, with the assumption that proper socialization would make for proper citizens. Still others put the greatest emphasis on vocational training, with the hope that immigrants would stay in school for more extended periods of time—and, in the process, become Americanized—if they were able to learn practical, job-related skills.[12] In most cases, public schools combined elements of all these curricular approaches in their attempt to integrate immigrant children into the "American" fold as efficiently as possible.

Given that the public school presented itself to immigrants as the dominant American medium for national identity, economic prosperity, and overall wellbeing, the lure of public schooling was, in many immigrant circles, irresistible. To be sure, not all groups took to the schools with equal enthusiasm. Devout Catholics, for example, sought to retain their children's loyalty to the Church and to protect their minds and souls from Protestant or highly secularized influences. They withdrew from public schools in large numbers, and the Church set up a separate, full-fledged parochial school apparatus.[13] Similarly, a small group of traditional observant and religious Orthodox Jews also opted to create private exclusively Jewish schools. Among most immigrant Jews at the turn of the twentieth century, however, public schooling was conceived of as nothing less than a great liberator.

In pre-Emancipation Europe, where state-sponsored schools subjected Jews to severe quotas, the responsibility for providing an education to Jewish children fell almost entirely on the Jewish community. Not surprisingly, it was common for Jewish schools to concentrate their efforts primarily on Jewish studies, for having religious knowledge was a sign of Jewish commitment as well as a functional necessity for everyday Jewish observance. But the *Haskalah* (Jewish Enlightenment) of the eighteenth century (Germany) and nineteenth century (Russia) opened "enlightened" Jews to the value of modern teachings and the notion of secular education as a means of social advancement in the wider society. Some European Jewish schools began to modernize their curricula and include secular content alongside Judaic subject matter.

Even so, attaining a full-blown secular education remained elusive for the majority of Europe's Jews—though their desires for secular learning were not dampened. In fact, for growing numbers of modernizing

Jews—particularly those who were open-minded enough to leave the often still-insular communities of the Old World and pursue a new life in America—acquiring a secular education remained an unfulfilled dream and a major desideratum.[14] For this reason, upon arrival in the United States most Jews zealously embraced their newfound right to attend public schools. There was a strong consensus among Jewish immigrants that public education was the key to social improvement, civic participation, and material success. Immigrant Jews saw Americanization and upward mobility as inherently entwined, and the promise of the American Dream was attributed to no institution more consistently than the public schools. The enthusiasm and earnestness with which immigrant Jews took up American public schooling quickly became the stuff of legend.

Indeed, few aspects of the American Jewish experience have been trumpeted as widely as the Jews' immersion in public schooling, especially for the sake of rapid advancement into the American middle class. Explanations of the Jews' so-called love affair with public schools often focus on certain pre-migration cultural attributes and ethnic behaviors—such as the Jews' renowned status as the "People of the Book" and their extensive experience with commerce and finance—that put them at an academic and economic advantage once they arrived on the American scene. Historian Leonard Dinnerstein argues that "there can be no doubt that educational endeavors must be regarded as a significant, if not the prime, cause of [the Jews'] social mobility. And the reason that education played this role was the high regard for learning that had for centuries pervaded the Jewish culture."[15]

Historian Penny Schine Gold refines this argument further by noting that Jews' centuries-long devotion to Jewish education was actually a devotion to religious education, and not secular education, so a transmutation of values seems to have occurred. In the Old World, Gold argues, Jews sought out knowledge of Jewish texts and tradition for the intrinsic rewards of that knowledge. By contrast, in the New World Jews sought out secular education for the extrinsic rewards it offered. Thus, "parents transferred their delight in the educational achievement of their children from the [Old World] heder and yeshivah to the [New World] public school and university," for secular education "facilitated entry into the intellectual, economic, and even social spheres of the dominant culture."[16] Statistics from the City College of New York indicate that more than half the enrollees in the first three decades of the twentieth century were Jewish, and the majority of Jewish men who graduated became doctors, lawyers, or teachers.[17] By excelling in school and entering into prestigious professions, second-generation immigrant Jews could not only satisfy their yearnings for a more comfortable existence, but also fulfill their immigrant parents' aspirations for status and acceptance within the wider society.[18]

Whether the Jews' rapid economic advancement was actually a product of their traditional reverence for learning and their successful use of public schools, or whether it can be attributed more appropriately to a host of other factors (e.g., entrepreneurship), has been debated extensively among historians and social scientists of American Jewry.[19] Sociologist Selma Berrol argues that public education could not have been the true facilitator of upward mobility for immigrant Jews, for the majority of Jews who attended public school in the early twentieth century did not receive an extended education beyond elementary school. In New York City in the 1900s and 1910s, there was a significant drop-off in the number of Jews who continued on from elementary school to junior high school, only a small number of Jews attended high schools, and only a portion of Jewish college students actually completed their degrees. Thus, although most Jews took advantage of public schooling, many children ultimately needed to leave school behind in their teenage years in order to financially support their families. In the final analysis, according to Berrol, second-generation Jews who received an extended education were only perpetuating the mobility already achieved by the enterprising first generation. After all, Jewish children would not have been able to acquire extensive academic training throughout their adolescence unless their families could afford the loss of the child's contribution to the household income.[20]

Be that as it may, most Jewish immigrants at least *perceived* public schools as ladders of upward mobility, and they took advantage of them accordingly. Unlike in Tsarist Russia, where those Jewish children who attended state schools were Russified and then denied the benefits of citizenship afterward, in America being Americanized in public schools appeared to have a concrete reward—equality of opportunity, if not equality of station. "Believing thoroughly in the wisdom of the fathers of the country in placing the public schools completely under the control of the State, the Jew contends that the school as a miniature republic is signally prepared to perform the great task of Americanization," wrote Rabbi Abram Simon of Washington Hebrew Congregation in 1912, capturing the prevailing sentiment of his day. "There is no greater friend of the American public school system than the Jew. There is none more eager to grasp its opportunities and none more grateful for its privileges."[21]

Still, public schooling also had its drawbacks. In the process of Americanizing students, teachers often denigrated Old World languages, customs, and allegiances. Even when teachers did not display an overt antagonism toward the immigrants' foreign traits, they still saw it as their duty to wean students away from their ethnic heritage as quickly as possible. Sometimes the cultural void left in the children would be filled with bald American patriotism—it was during this time, for example, that the Pledge of Allegiance, the "Star Spangled Banner," and salutes to the American flag became daily rituals in public school classrooms. Frequently, however, Americanization activities did more to delegitimize ethnic group identity than to actually promote a distinctly "American" identity. The so-called good American citizen that the public schools attempted to cultivate was one who overcame his or her commitment to collective group life and was instead willing to participate in the greater commonweal as an autonomous individual. Toward this end, acquiring "American" cultural practices and affects, though essential, still remained of secondary importance to jettisoning ethnic entanglements.[22]

Compounding the Americanization challenge to Jewish identification was the fact that public school teachers often linked American social mobility with an essentially Puritan ethos. Character lessons about obedience, industry, and temperance were decidedly Protestant in origin and thrust. Furthermore, despite the professed intention of public school reformers to make the schools more secular and despite vociferous opposition to Protestant teachings mounted by Catholics and Jews, it was still fairly common for selections from the King James Bible to be read aloud and for Protestant prayers to be recited in public school classrooms. Historian Kate Rousmaniere notes that "Jewish teachers often worked where there was a common assumption of Christian cultural knowledge, and they heard Christian readings at daily assemblies, learned and taught Christian songs, and produced Christmas pageants"—all of which were construed as ordinary practices in America's public schools well into the twentieth century.[23]

A final dilemma of public schooling was that it precipitated a gulf between acculturated children and their immigrant parents. The public schools placed a heavy emphasis on instilling proper behaviors, morals, hygiene, etiquette, and taste, so that the purportedly "backward" lifestyles of their immigrant charges could be ameliorated. It was then expected that "American" students would transform their "foreign" homes by imparting good manners to their extended families.[24] Although the fraternal bonds of the immigrant family unit remained rather strong—given that the family often lived in cramped quarters, everyone contributed in one way or another to the household economy, and parents doted on their children in order to help them along the ladder of mobility—Americanized children predictably began to look at their Old World parents—or at least their parents' Old World customs—disparagingly. Summing up the estrangement between Jewish children and parents that could result from Americanization programs in the public schools, Isaac Berkson, a leading Jewish educator in the 1910s–1930s, observed:

> Having gained a public school education and speaking English (with a New York, not a foreign accent), they tend to regard themselves superior to their parents and everything associated with them.... They have lost whatever culture was inherent in the customs and institutions of their parents' traditional life.[25]

With second-generation American Jews increasingly abandoning the traditions of their parents, the continuity of the Jewish community on the American scene appeared to be in grave danger. The dual nature of public schooling—which could be beneficial to Jewish individuals, as it empowered them to achieve social, economic, and political status, but detrimental to the Jewish community, as it helped to break down bonds between children and their ethno-religious group—created a crisis of adjustment that American Jewish leaders felt needed to be addressed. "The form and content of Judaism and Jewish culture in this land will depend largely on the system of Jewish education with which we provide the rising generation of Jews," proclaimed Julius Greenstone, head of Gratz College's Jewish teacher training program, in an article for the *American Jewish Yearbook*. "This is a great responsibility and also a glorious opportunity. To realize this opportunity to its fullest extent and to set to work to discharge the responsibility to the best of our abilities is the duty of American Israel at the present time."[26]

The Creation of a Culture of American Jewish Schooling

Jewish schooling was already a fixture in American Jewish life, from the founding of the first synagogue-based school in the eighteenth century, to the development of all-day Jewish denominational schools by the early nineteenth century, to the expansion of the Jewish Sunday school movement at mid-century, to the emergence of supplementary Jewish schooling among eastern European Jews by the turn of the twentieth century.[27] The efficacy of Jewish schooling had been challenged at various times by a lack of resources, space, materials, personnel, pupils, direction, vision, and talent, as well as by the Americanizing proclivities of the immigrant populace. Nonetheless, the American Jewish education enterprise was hardly a non-entity when the issue of Jewish schooling reemerged on the communal agenda in the early twentieth century.

The majority of American Jews, however, were not entirely convinced that any sort of Jewish schooling was worthwhile. The various advantages of public schooling over Jewish schooling were manifest: (1) Attendance at public schools was compulsory and free, while attendance at Jewish schools was voluntary and often fee-based. (2) Public schools offered the practical skills necessary for advancement in the liberal, free market, democratic society, while Jewish schools only offered the chance to be a standout in Judaic knowledge within the community. (3) Public schooling normally took place in new, clean, well-furnished, technologically advanced, architecturally impressive buildings, while Jewish schooling commonly took place in the basements of synagogues, on the ground floors of tenements, in the backs of shops or saloons, in living rooms and kitchens, or wherever else an itinerant teacher could assemble a group of pupils. (4) Public schools had boundless resources from the state while Jewish school finances were precarious at best. (5) Most public school teachers were trained in up-to-date pedagogical methods, had a decent command of their subject matter areas, and were provided with a livable wage, while most Jewish teachers relied mainly on rudimentary instructional techniques to teach Judaic subjects they sometimes barely knew and for little or no pay. For all these reasons, young, aspiring, wide-eyed Jewish immigrant children like Mary Antin were prone to look upon American schools as the "apex of [their] civic pride and personal contentment" and to look back on Old World Jewish schools as "gray within and without."[28]

What is more, the immigrants' drive to enter the middle class not only meant that parents worked long hours, but also that, after attending public school in the mornings, most children worked in the afternoons, evenings, or on weekends, so they had little time for Jewish schooling. In addition, the lures of cosmopolitan urban life—summarized by one observer as "the street corner, the movies, the baseball scores and musical comedy"—were particularly strong for young people.[29] Second-generation American Jews were keenly aware that Jewish living in America was a choice. While most children would continue to opt into the community for the sake of loyalty, collectivity, security, or nostalgia, many would choose to opt out as well.[30] It appeared that Jewish schools simply could not compete for their students' time or attention.

In a 1913 study for the US Department of Education on "The Problem of Jewish Education for the Children of Immigrants," Israel Friedlander, a professor of Bible and education at the Jewish Theological Seminary, observed: "The Jewish home which had always been the power house of the Jewish religion lost most of its influence as an educational factor among the Jewish people."[31] Perhaps no statement better captures the essence of the culture of American Jewish schooling that evolved in response to these circumstances.

Distressed by the fact that many immigrant Jews, in their drive to enter the American mainstream, shied away from observing Jewish customs and participating in Jewish institutions, communal leaders were convinced that the best means for preserving Jewish life on the American scene was to shift responsibility for Jewish education from the home and sanctuary to the Jewish school. To this end, they developed a system of part-time Jewish supplementary schools that, like public schools, could adequately serve *in loco parentis*. In this case, the new format of Jewish supplementary schools would instill in children the knowledge, means, and will to live Jewishly in the democratic, pluralistic, secular context. Many Jewish educators saw their task as creating an intensified Jewish cultural environment in the supplementary schools, so that future generations of American Jews ultimately would be inspired to retain ties to their ethnic group and religious faith. Moreover, Jewish educators felt it was their distinct moral and professional responsibility to effectuate the development of Jewish attachments among the rising generation—and thereby ensure the continuity of the American Jewish community—for most Jewish parents were failing to accomplish these aims on their own. In the end, it was Jewish supplementary schooling in which most communal leaders put their faith as the future of American Judaism.

The idea that formal Jewish schooling should supplement and enhance the informal Jewish education children received at home was not novel. To the contrary, through the ages Jewish academies, teachers, and tutors had assumed the primary communal responsibility for imparting knowledge of the Torah—its language, precepts, and interpretations—while parents and rabbis reinforced traditional Jewish customs, symbolic rituals, and religious commitments at home and in the synagogue. However, in the

American context, as both the home and the synagogue began to lose their influence on acculturating Jews, Jewish supplementary schooling took on a special urgency. By serving *in loco parentis* and assuming roles that once had been almost exclusively the province of the Jewish home—for example, teaching children how and why to celebrate Jewish holidays—Jewish educators ostensibly would be able to protect the increasingly secularized and Americanized Jewish community from itself. As Samson Benderly, founding director of the Bureau of Jewish Education of New York City (est. 1910), put it, "what is by long odds ... most important, is how to find the right way of interesting our children in the observance of our beautiful ceremonies, thus indirectly re-Judaizing the Jewish home and bringing back the parents."[32] Accordingly, the traditional obligation and function of parents in providing for the Jewish education of their children was turned on its head. No longer could the community rely on the Jewish home to impart Jewish values. Rather, it would be left primarily to the school, working in conjunction with other community institutions and organizations, to perpetuate Jewish life.

In this scheme, neither the Old World *melamdim* (didacts) of the *heders*, *talmud torahs*, and *yeshivas*, who often were well-versed in Judaic subjects but lacking in curricular imagination and pedagogical skill, nor the Protestant-style nineteenth-century Jewish Sunday schools, which focused on inspirational moral and religious dicta from the Bible, would suffice for modern American Jewish supplementary schooling. The type of Jewish instruction children now needed went well beyond the mechanics of reading Hebrew prayers and memorizing biblical passages. Instead, American Jewish educators would need to serve as role models for modern Jewish living on the American scene. New American Jews brought with them more secular Jewish sensibilities grounded in a rich ethnic and cultural heritage of Jewish food, stories, song, dance, art, comedy, criticism, language, journalism, politics, Zionism, peoplehood, and values. To capture the attention of these new American Jews, cultural, linguistic, ethnic, and national expression would need to be the focal point of Jewish educational activity, rather than traditional religious instruction exclusively.

Furthermore, because the public school was viewed by Jewish immigrants as the entryway to American society *sine qua non*, any form of Jewish education would need to be complementary to this pursuit. Practically speaking, the calendaring of the public school meant that the most viable option for Jewish schooling was after school and/or on weekends. Thus, most Jewish schools were (and still are) part-time afternoon or weekend schools, known alternatively as "supplementary school," "Hebrew school," "religious school," "synagogue school," "Sunday school," or "complementary school," taking place anywhere from one to six hours a week, on one or more days of the week, over the course of one to six years, typically up till *bar/bat mitzvah*.

Conceptually speaking, being complementary to public schools meant that Jewish schools needed to be in line with their format, pedagogy, and ethos in order to make the children's educational experiences continuous and harmonious. Thus, paradoxically enough, public schooling would become the exemplar of what Jewish schooling should be. Modern American Jewish supplementary schools would emphasize a program of social education, or really Judaization, that in parallel to Americanization programs in public schools emphasized Jewish heritage, heroes, holidays, ethics, rituals, foundational texts, culture, Israel, and Hebrew language, and would thereby teach young Jews to be good, proud, active citizens of the American and the American Jewish community.[33] Alongside or sometimes in place of expertise in Jewish text study, the new competencies Jewish educators would require ranged from teaching *Ivrit b'Ivrit* (a method of learning Hebrew by speaking Hebrew), to designing hands-on Jewish holiday and *tzedakah* (philanthropy and social justice) projects, to leading Jewish songs and dances, and much more, all in line with the new wisdom of progressive pedagogy that emphasized child-centered, activity-oriented, inquiry-based instruction. Above all, Jewish teachers would need to be knowledgeable, enthusiastic, energetic, and talented enough to inspire in American Jewish children a fresh commitment to Jewish identity and continuity.[34]

Like America's public schools, which were controlled by local and state authorities and lacked a national curriculum or federal structure, the new American Jewish school system reflected a localized model in which the schools were the exclusive responsibility of local synagogues, bureaus of Jewish education, and community federations, along with their professional and lay leadership. The American Jewish education enterprise was in fact a loosely coupled system of confederated entities that were bound together by similar goals, subject matters, and approaches, but otherwise totally lacking in coherence, coordination, superstructure, and policy.[35]

The education departments of national Jewish denominational organizations such as the Union of American Hebrew Congregations (now Union of Reform Judaism) and the United Synagogue of America (now United Synagogue of Conservative Judaism), as well as umbrella Jewish education organizations such as the American Association for Jewish Education

(AAJE) and the Jewish Education Service of North America (JESNA), advised local schools on mission, content, organization, and practices, but their recommendations were non-binding. Other entities that have exerted extensive influence on the shape of American Jewish schooling include Jewish education scholars and training institutes (e.g., teachers' colleges such as Gratz College in Philadelphia and Hebrew College in Boston; denominational seminaries such as Hebrew Union College-Jewish Institute of Religion in Los Angeles and the Jewish Theological Seminary and Yeshiva University in New York; and later secular universities such as Brandeis University and New York University), Jewish publishing houses (e.g., the Jewish Publication Society, Ktav, Behrman House, Torah Aura), Jewish education consultancies (e.g., Partnership for Excellence in Jewish Education), denominational and community day school associations (now merged into one overarching network, Prizmah), and Jewish family foundations and philanthropies (e.g., Melton, Mandel, Bronfman, AVI CHAI, Steinhardt, Jim Joseph, Schusterman). But these influences, while significant, were mostly piecemeal or sporadic and not systemic.

For the most part, the success of American Jewish schooling relied on the talents of a few select individuals in a few select places: in the early twentieth century, the disciples of Samson Benderly at New York's Bureau of Jewish Education who went on to establish a network of bureaus and departments of Jewish education in cities nationwide; at mid-century, an elite group of outstanding pulpit rabbis and rabbi-educators who served large, noteworthy congregations across the country; and toward the end of the century, powerful and dynamic heads of day schools. In contrast to the public school system, however, which was massive enough to collectively marshal considerable political clout and financial resources for large-scale curriculum projects, teacher preparation and licensure programs, research and development initiatives, and building and infrastructure improvements, the American Jewish supplementary school system remained underdeveloped, under-resourced, and siloed.

While American Jewish schooling was radically localized, the essential characteristics of these schools—mission statements, curriculum, staffing, facilities, resources, parents, students—were relatively common, and they shared common predicaments as well. Where they diverged, especially, was with respect to vision. Some school stakeholders felt that Jewish supplementary schooling was meant foremost to teach young Jews how to be Jewish and expected the supplementary schools to teach Jewish literacy, behaviors, and dispositions. Others believed in educating Jewish youth to retain links with their Jewish heritage and practice the Jewish way of life, although the meaning of the terms "retain links," "Jewish heritage," and "Jewish way of life" was vague. The only thing certain for these stakeholders was that children should emerge from Jewish schools with strong "Jewish identity." Another group of stakeholders was interested in shifting the emphasis of schooling from "Judaism" the religion to "Jews" the people, and they wanted to focus on the present situation of America's Jews and the State of Israel. This group was especially interested in guaranteeing "Jewish continuity," a term that meant Jewish survival but was also a code word for endogamy. On the other hand, within the context of the post-World War II and Will Herberg's *Protestant-Catholic-Jew* (first published in 1955) milieu, some Reform, Conservative, and Reconstructionist rabbis and movement-based educators advocated for teaching the main tenets of their denominations, along with religious values clarification exercises and lessons on comparative religion.[36] Still another group of Jewish parents cared little about Jewish literacy, identity, continuity, or faith, and instead dropped their kids off at school for the express purpose of preparing them for *bar/bat mitzvah*. These children started Jewish schooling shortly before the *bar/bat mitzvah* years (whenever required by the school) and ended it the day after the *bar/bat mitzvah*; these parents had little interest in or concern about whatever else was covered in the curriculum. Ultimately, the shaping dilemma of American Jewish supplementary schooling derived (and derives) from the search for an answer to the question, "Jewish education for what?," which shapes all aspects of education: what to teach; how to teach; who should teach; to whom; where; and for what outcomes.[37]

This diversity of visions and practices led to a broad canvas of curricula, programming, and frameworks in supplementary schools. Hebrew was initially taught as a language of the prayer book and also a spoken language of the Jewish people. By mid-twentieth century, however, the latter task was found to be overly burdensome for such a part-time school setting, so the main focus of Hebrew instruction became basic language decoding for ritual purposes. The Bible historically had been taught as a core text of the Jewish people expressing foundational religious and moral ideas and also as an entryway to sophisticated biblical and rabbinic textual interpretation. But with only a few hours of contact time per week, teaching Bible in supplementary schools became the cursory review of selective chapters, stories, and principles from the Five Books of Moses and the Prophets. The teaching of Jewish rituals in the school was essentially a new

American invention, considering that in the Old World these practices had been demonstrated regularly to children at home and in the synagogue so they did not need be covered in the curriculum. The formalization of the subject matter in lessons on "Customs and Ceremonies" and "Jewish Life" deprived the rituals of their intimacy, relevance, and vibrancy. The study of Jewish history and social studies was once a central feature of the Judaization project of American Jewish supplementary schools, but it ultimately was squeezed out of the curriculum by a drive toward *bar/bat mitzvah* preparation and a reluctance to confront the complicated nuances of Jewish past and current events.

Ultimately, in most cases, the course of study in Jewish supplementary schools was shaped by the Jewish calendar. In the fall, the subject was the high holidays; in the winter, it was Hanukkah, Tu B'Shevat, and Purim; and in the spring, it was Passover and Lag Ba'Omer. (It can fairly be assumed that one reason Shavuot is the least celebrated major Jewish holiday in America is that it normally comes in the late spring when the school season is over, so few schools cover it.) Clearly, the greatest challenge in curricularizing the Jewish supplementary school was the massive scope of Jewish civilization that ostensibly needed to be covered in only a few hours of instruction.

What is more, while each or all of these diverse Jewish school topics might have been of interest and often engaging, it was not always clear how they customarily fit together. When confronted with the question, "What is taught to you in Hebrew school?," the child might list the holidays, some Hebrew words, some values, some biblical heroes, and some major events, but in the end these respective topics were somewhat of a hodge-podge, so that many students were left with no coherent sense of Judaism or Jewish civilization. Compounding the problem was the sporadic school schedule, in which classes met either once or a few times per week, and they were preempted by events on the Jewish, secular, or personal family calendar. With such irregular attendance, even in the best of conditions it was difficult for teachers to plan an adequate curricular scope and sequence. While educators may have intended to teach their subject matters with increasing depth and sophistication, in reality they had very limited time for rather lofty goals.[38] Given the circumstances, the anticipated psychological and sociological outcomes of supplementary schools—Jewish literacy, Jewish identification, Jewish living, Jewish continuity, and the like—were destined to fall short of expectations.

Perhaps no facet of supplementary Jewish schooling suffered more from the part-time nature of the enterprise than the quality of its teaching force.

The synagogue rabbi was typically the titular head of the school, while stewardship was assigned to a full-time professional Jewish educator who was responsible for scheduling, curriculum development, staffing, professional development, board and parent relations, student supervision, and evaluation. The rest of the faculty consisted of part-time educators who taught a few hours per week on Sundays and/or in evenings, were paid little to nothing with no fringe benefits, and had little to no formal teacher training or subject matter knowledge. Although Jewish teachers' colleges collectively produced dozens of knowledgeable, capable, energetic, mission-driven professional educators per year, they mostly went into administrative positions in the schools, leaving the thousands of classrooms to be staffed by those with little training. This makeshift teaching force consisted of native Hebrew speakers who themselves were new arrivals to the United States; knowledgeable and involved lay people eager to serve their congregations by teaching religious school; traditionalist Jews with strong backgrounds in Hebrew and Jewish texts who wanted to supplement their income; and university students with majors or minors in Judaic studies. To be sure, over the years, many competent, awe-inspiring, memorable supplementary school teachers successfully shaped young people's lives. But for the most part, the Jewish teaching profession was fundamentally constrained by a lack of adequate training, credentialing, supervision, remuneration, and respect. Supplementary schools would flounder accordingly.

The supplementary school model became much maligned in American Jewish culture because, in the end, it simply could not compete with the other priorities—educational, occupational, recreational, and otherwise—of mainstream American Jewry. Over the past century, copious resources, energies, and talents have been poured into the supplementary school system in an attempt to prop it up at the very least and in many cases to improve it significantly. Recent initiatives coming out of the Reform movement especially, such as the Experiment in Congregational Education, the B'nai Mitzvah Revolution, and the creation of full-time Hebrew school faculty positions at places like Central Synagogue in New York City, have given new life to supplementary schools. Less consideration has been given to the question of whether the supplementary school model ought to be sustained altogether. Indeed, Hebrew school is so ingrained in American Jewish culture and synagogue life that any prospect of moving forward without it is seemingly beyond imagination.

AN ALTERNATIVE MODEL FOR JEWISH SCHOOLING: THE DAY SCHOOL

Supplementary Jewish schools were not the only form of American Jewish schooling to rise to prominence in the twentieth century. A confluence of mid-century circumstances, including increased ambivalence among the general populace about the efficacy of public education; the mandatory effort to desegregate America's public schools; the shifting demographics of urban and suburban areas and their schools; the growing financial, political, and social stability of the American Jewish community; and the desire among many Jews for a richer Jewish educational experience than supplementary Jewish schools provided, prompted a small but influential group of American Jews in the 1950s and 1960s to opt for an alternative educational framework—the day school—which would combine Jewish and general studies in an all-day private school setting. While day schools would never become the mainstream American Jewish educational framework (in recent years, only about 18% of all American Jewish children attended day schools annually, and 80% of those children were Orthodox Jews who have long opted for traditionalist yeshivas over public schools), the day school nonetheless became a significant format, frequently heralded by its advocates as the key to Jewish survival and continuity on the American scene.[39]

The day school was shaped by the grammar of American schooling perhaps even more than the supplementary school had been. After all, it needed to meet all the general studies curriculum standards, school laws, and administrative regulations mandated by the local and state education boards that governed, evaluated, and accredited it. In many cases, general studies teachers in Jewish day schools were expected (though not required) to have the same certification credentials as public school teachers. The Jewish day school was typically housed in a structure that physically and symbolically imitated the architecture of the public school and schools with adequate resources and contained the full complement of classrooms, administrative offices, nurse's and guidance offices, science labs, libraries, cafeterias and gymnasiums, athletic fields, music and art rooms, theatrical stages, and special needs resource rooms. Put simply, the modern Jewish day school looks and functions like a typical American school.[40]

In addition, the day school functions as a private school. Private schools actually pre-date public schools in America, as schooling was not government-sponsored and compulsory till the mid- to late-nineteenth century, while denominational and grammar schools had existed since the arrival of the first European settlers in the seventeenth century. With the expansion of public education in the early twentieth century also came an expansion of non-public schools, dedicated to an alternative ethos and funded by a mix of private tuition, investments, and philanthropy. The American private school system included a powerful network of Catholic schools, as well as a small group of elite independent schools and residential academies. Private schools had to comply with the basic requirements of American schooling, including its core academic subjects, administrative mechanisms, and health and safety standards. But they could be altogether different from public schools in their mission, supporting subjects, pedagogies, activities, and constituencies. Thus, private schools offered an educational framework in which special interest groups could provide schooling that would simultaneously accommodate the norms of public schooling and the sponsoring group's distinct needs.

From the outset, the Jewish day school did not target the same audience as the elite private schools, for it was an institution dedicated to a specific demographic: namely, Jews interested in enhancing the Jewish literacy and Jewish connection of their children. The Jewish day school focused on a sector of American Jewry seeking both a rigorous general education and more intense study of Jewish heritage than that provided by supplementary schools. The first function of Jewish day schooling, then, was providing an expanded Jewish learning experience. Rather than one to six hours of Jewish instruction per week, as with the supplementary schools, day schools could provide 15 hours or more of Jewish instruction per week. The shapers of the modern Jewish day school also learned that the key to success was the creation of schools that also provided the highest quality general education, so as to adequately compete with public as well as (non-sectarian) private schooling, and to facilitate the advancement of Jewish children toward higher education and professional careers. As a result, another one of the main functions of Jewish day schools, particularly on the high school level, quickly became college preparation. Finally, private schools are known for their exclusivity, their circumscribed social networks, and their unique school cultures, all of which foster a cooperative spirit and a sense of belonging among their constituents. Accordingly, a third major function of Jewish day schools was the creation of a bounded and bonded community of Jewish children, parents, educators, and stakeholders committed to full-time Jewish education and, by extension, the perpetuation of Jewish life.

As to the curriculum, the general education of the day school encompassed the standard subject areas of American schools: English language arts, sciences, mathematics, social studies, and other subjects (e.g., languages, arts, physical education) variously mandated by local authorities. In addition, the day school provided enhanced teaching of Jewish topics: Bible, Hebrew, Jewish texts, Jewish ceremonies and observances, prayer book and synagogue skills, Jewish history, Jewish values and beliefs, and Israel. The two spheres of knowledge that constituted the curriculum of the day school came to be popularly known as "the dual curriculum," referring to two core bodies of knowledge regarded as important for being a well-educated twentieth-century American and Jew. The educational vision of the dual-curriculum day school was that students could master these differing but complementary intellectual and cultural domains together and under one comprehensive program.

This vision of Jewish education is at the heart of *The Cannibal Galaxy*, Cynthia Ozick's 1986 novel that traces the story of a Jewish day school located "in mid-century, Midwest middling America."[41] The protagonist, Joseph Brill, the founder of the school, is a Jew of eastern European descent who had earlier lived in the heavily Jewish district of the Marais (or as it was commonly known by its Yiddish name, "the Pletzel," meaning little square) in Paris. Brill was torn between his insular Jewish roots and the grand cosmopolitan museums, libraries, and culture of Paris. The exigencies of history resulted in Brill hiding in the cellar of a Catholic convent during the Nazi invasion, surrounded by tomes of the world's great thinkers. One day in the cellar of the convent, writes Ozick,

> Brill was shot through by his idea. If they did not hunt him, if he lived, if the war ended, and he survived it, he would be a teacher and marry and unite his two minds... So it came to pass that Joseph Brill imprisoned in a school vowed that he would found a school—a school run according to the principle of twin nobilities, twin antiquities. The fusion of scholarly Europe and burnished Jerusalem. The grace of Madame de Sevigne's flowery courtyard mated to the perfect serenity of a purified Sabbath. Corneille and Racine set beside Jonah and Koheleth... He saw the civilization that invented the telescope side by side with the civilization that invented conscience. Astronomers and God-praisers united in majestic peace.[42]

Brill ultimately reaches America and creates such a day school, the Edmond Fleg Primary School.[43] This school is rooted in his notion of the "twin nobilities," which Brill considers to be his unique inspiration. The book traces the emergence but gradual demise of Brill's dream. By the end of the book, Brill is in retirement in a Florida condominium and the name of the Edmond Fleg Primary School has been changed to the Lakeside Grade School.

Ozick's novel points to the challenges that ultimately thwarted the dream of the twin nobilities in day schools. She depicts meddlesome parents who came to school regularly to complain about the lunch schedule, math workbooks, and student stress levels; teachers who seemingly were not capable of understanding, teaching, or even really caring about either or both of the twin nobilities, so that the grandeur of both Jewish and general studies was lost on the students; Jewish educators whose classes degenerate into the boring pedagogies and skill sets of the old-style *heder*; and students who just don't get it. The dream of the dual curriculum remained ephemeral and, in her novel, increasingly was regarded as the pipe dream of an aging eccentric foreign-born Jewish educator. The all-powerful American educational culture eventually swallows up the smaller planet of Jewish knowledge, like a cannibal galaxy that devours the weaker celestial bodies in its reach. At the novel's end, the hope of teaching two cultures seeking a viable co-existence proved to be harder than expected.

Indeed, the grand vision of the dual curriculum has proved to be overly ambitious for many Jewish day schools. Underlying epistemological questions regarding the teaching of Jewish and general studies were not easily answered: Are Jewish and general learning methodologically similar? Are they really parallel or are they in fact entirely different types of knowledge? What pedagogical content knowledge is distinct to each of these realms, and what feasibly crosses over?[44] How can teachers be trained to teach both of these faculties? Are the twin nobilities actually equivalent in status?[45]

The modern Orthodox day school resolved some of these questions by referring to general studies as *limudei chol* (secular studies) and Jewish studies as *limudei kodesh* (sacred studies)—terminology that is both descriptive and pejorative. *Limudei chol* were taught by highly qualified teachers in specific secular subject areas and were aimed at the highest levels of academic achievement and advancement. *Limudei kodesh* were taught by rabbis and Jewish educators who had deep knowledge of Jewish sources while also being exemplars of Orthodox Jewish lifestyle. This structure called for excellence in all areas while establishing a clear hierarchy between the general, which was mundane, and the Jewish, which was holy.

The relationship of Jewish and general studies in non-Orthodox Jewish day schools has been more complicated. General studies are regarded as essential for understanding the world at-large and for the ability to advance in American society. General subjects are taught by full-time, often licensed, usually highly skilled teachers, many of whom earned advanced university degrees in their respective subject areas. The overarching goal of general education in non-Orthodox day schools is mastery of core school subject matter. (In Jewish high schools, an added incentive is proof of this mastery on standardized tests—e.g., Advanced Placement and College Board exams—and superlative transcripts that will improve college entrance prospects.) Jewish studies are regarded as instrumental to understanding Jewish heritage and deepening Jewish identification. These subjects are taught by full-time Jewish educators, some of whom have rabbinic ordination or advanced degrees in Jewish studies, who are either fluent in Hebrew (often Israeli transplants), knowledgeable about Jewish subject matter, and/or deeply concerned about the Jewish future.

The intended outcome of day schooling has been self-consciously identified young American Jews. Although ostensibly general studies and Jewish studies carry equal weight in non-Orthodox day schools, the hierarchies are in reality just subtler and reversed. In these day schools, some of which compete with the finest public and private schools, preparation for secular high schools and colleges is of paramount concern (most day schools are elementary and middle school level, though there are several venerable day high schools). These day schools would not necessarily be endangered if the majority of their graduates failed Jewish studies exams, though that would certainly be cause for distress. However, they would most likely falter if the majority of their graduates ultimately failed to matriculate and succeed at respectable high schools and prestigious universities.

The dual-curriculum Jewish day school has proved to be very successful in creating a framework in which two cultures could be taught at once, but less successful in resolving the complex dynamics of the twin nobilities and their implications. The Code of Hammurabi might be taught in the elementary grades as an important document in the emergence of secular Western law, government, and civilization, while the Five Books of Moses are likely to be presented as God's word, a call for ethical behavior, and proof of God's promise of the Land of Israel to the Jewish people.[46] A high school class on world history in the fall semester might focus on political, economic, and moral aspects of World War I and its impact on the outbreak of World War II, while a course on modern Jewish history in the spring semester might include a unit on the uniqueness of the Holocaust as a product of rabid anti-Semitism, in no way connected to the themes of the fall course. The sense often emerges that general studies are aimed at thinking while Jewish studies are aimed at believing.[47]

The actual daily life of the typical dual-curriculum modern Jewish day school is populated by Jews and non-Jews (teachers, staff, some students);

celebrations of American, Israeli, and Jewish holidays alike; competitive sports with local Jewish and non-Jewish private schools; classic American musicals sometimes presented in Hebrew; and other hybrids of American and Jewish civilizations. In this way, day schools have been able to create a both Jewish and American atmosphere at once. At the same time, intelligent students in day schools often experience two distinct selves: a Jewish self in morning classes and a general self in afternoon classes, figuratively speaking. While this arrangement may reflect the quintessential expression of modern Jewish identity—"Be a Jew at home and a man on the street," as the eighteenth-century enlightenment Jewish thinker Moses Mendelsohn phrased it—the bifurcation does not accord with the fundamentally entwined nature of post-modern American Jewish life today. In the end, the modern American Jewish day school is usually a successful private school that offers an immersive Jewish atmosphere, but it is less likely to engage its students in the deep implications of conjoining the twin nobilities.

Culture and Counterculture

The two main twentieth-century formats for American Jewish schooling—the supplementary school and the day school—reflect the achievements and challenges of creating a modern system of Jewish education in the American context. The greatest achievement of the supplementary school has been its endurance over the past century. While it has been a beleaguered system, with its often ambiguous aims, uneven curricula, paltry teaching, loose structure, and limitations of time, it appears to have nonetheless satisfied most American Jews' desires and needs for some modicum of Jewish education. Indeed, to this day, the majority of America's Jews are products of supplementary schools. Moreover, the supplementary school system has always been receptive to serious reform efforts, to the extent that supplementary schools are frequently trailblazers in Jewish educational innovation in any given time and place. For its part, the achievement of the day school system has been its ability to create a school that rivals some of the best public and private schools in their geographic area while also fostering among its constituents a sense of Jewish community and continuity. Its challenges have included recruitment, affordability, staffing, and a lack of curricular consonance between general and Jewish studies. But to its credit, a significant percentage of contemporary American Jewish communal leaders attended Orthodox or non-Orthodox day schools, demonstrating the value of the system not only for college preparation, but also for communal perpetuation.[48]

In recent decades, there has been increased interest among communal leadership and philanthropists in the improvement of American Jewish schooling. The discussion normally has focused on what sorts of momentous and transformative Jewish experiences for youth will lead to adult Jewish involvement. This thinking has been fostered by a classic Jewish sociological impact study model that regards Jewish schooling as the input (independent variable) and adult Jewish endogamy, organizational affiliation, and/or Jewish ritual participation as signs of the success or failure of schooling (dependent variables). Yet we know from decades of general educational research that correlational studies between education and adult achievement are difficult to interpret as causational. There are a host of social, economic, and other factors over and above schooling that shape adult identity, so correlation and causation is nearly impossible to pinpoint.

The causational theory becomes even more complicated in Jewish life where there is no agreed upon notion of what the desired outcomes are. In one renowned study of the impact of childhood Jewish educational experiences on adult Jewish involvement, the researchers found that seven or more years of day schooling was the best guarantor of Jewish in-marriage, while those children who attended Sunday school were more likely to marry outside the faith than those who received no Jewish schooling at all (though in most other measures, some schooling came out on top)![49] Some Jewish educators have reservations about this impact study model and have developed alternative research approaches that attempt to identify the qualities of good schools and best practices that might lead to improved learning environments in day and supplementary schools.[50]

Impact studies also have led to the search for new alternatives to Jewish schooling, such as summer camps, cultural activities, and Israel travel, that might offer more efficient, more economical, and/or more conclusive outcomes than schooling. Some of these initiatives hearken back to pioneering ventures that originated in the 1910s–1950s (e.g., alternative Jewish after-school programs), while others are singular products of the twenty-first-century milieu (e.g., online Jewish gaming). These developments, each in its own way, may be called countercultural insofar as they are responses and alternatives to the dominant cultural framework of American Jewish schooling. Our discussion of the cultures of Jewish education continues in the next chapter with consideration of the countercultural trend in the contemporary American Jewish educational enterprise.

NOTES

1. Stephan F. Brumberg, *Going to America, Going to School: The Jewish Immigrant Public School Encounter in Turn-of-the-Century New York City* (New York: Praeger, 1986), 70. Emphases in the original.
2. Ibid., 3. It is important to note that the immigration of eastern European Jews was primarily that of families, not just employable young males; thus, a significant proportion of the Jewish immigrant population was comprised of school-age children.
3. Gil Graff, *"And You Shall Teach Them Diligently": A Concise History of Jewish Education in the United States, 1776–2000* (New York: Jewish Theological Seminary, 2008); Jonathan Woocher and Meredith Woocher, "American Jewish Education," in the *American Jewish Year Book 2014*, ed. Arnold Dashefsky and Ira M. Sheskin (New York: Springer, 2015).
4. David Schoem, *Ethnic Survival in America: An Ethnography of a Jewish Afternoon School* (Atlanta, GA: Scholars Press, 1989). See also Philip Roth, "The Conversion of the Jews," in *Goodbye Columbus* (New York: Vintage, 1994).
5. Lawrence A. Cremin, *American Education: The Metropolitan Experience, 1876–1980* (New York: Harper Collins, 1988), ix–x.
6. Sarah Mondale and Sarah B. Patton, eds., *School: The Story of American Public Education* (Boston: Beacon Press, 2001), x.
7. David B. Tyack and Larry Cuban, *Tinkering Toward Utopia: A Century of Public School Reform* (Cambridge, MA: Harvard University Press, 1995).
8. See Carl F. Kaestle, *Pillars of the Republic: Common Schools and American Society, 1780–1860* (New York: Hill and Wang, 1983); Lawrence A. Cremin, ed., *The Republic and the School: Horace Mann on the Education of Free Man*, Classics in Education No. 1 (New York: Teachers College Press, 1957), 3–28; David B. Tyack, *Seeking Common Ground: Public Schools in a Diverse Society* (Cambridge, MA: Harvard University Press, 2003). We will be using "American" as a blanket reference to what traditionally has been conceived of as the core culture/cultural group of the United States—Anglo-Saxon, Protestant, and middle-class.
9. For a general discussion of Americanization activities, see John Bodnar, *The Transplanted: A History of Immigrants in Urban America* (Bloomington: Indiana University Press, 1985).
10. See David B. Tyack, *The One Best System: A History of American Urban Education* (Cambridge, MA: Harvard University Press, 1974).
11. *New York Times*, "The Public Schools," September 11, 1894.
12. Reed Ueda, "Second-Generation Civic America: Education, Citizenship, and the Children of Immigrants," *Journal of Interdisciplinary History* 29, no. 4 (1999); Robert A. Carlson, *The Quest for Conformity: Americanization*

through Education (New York: John Wiley and Sons, 1975); Paula S. Fass, *Outside In: Minorities and the Transformation of American Education* (New York: Oxford University Press, 1989).

13. Joel Perlmann, *Ethnic Differences: Schooling and Social Structure among the Irish, Italians, Jews, and Blacks in an American City, 1880–1935* (New York: Cambridge University Press, 1988).

14. The American Jewish community is highly variegated and complex. It is unfeasible in this limited space to address all the variations in Jewish affiliation—religious, ethnic, political, social, and otherwise—that manifested themselves within the community during this period. The reader should keep in mind that, for the sake of brevity, American Jewish life is being described in broad terms here, even if such a move inevitably obscures the full range of the American Jewish experience.

15. Leonard Dinnerstein, "Education and the Advancement of American Jews," in *American Education and the European Immigrant, 1840–1940*, ed. Bernard J. Weiss (Urbana: University of Illinois Press, 1982), 44–46.

16. Penny Schine Gold, *Making the Bible Modern: Children's Bibles and Jewish Education in Twentieth-Century America* (Ithaca, NY: Cornell University Press, 2004), 70.

17. Selma C. Berrol, "Education and Economic Mobility: The Jewish Experience in New York City, 1880–1920," *American Jewish Historical Quarterly* 65, no. 3 (1976): 269. See also Mariam K. Slater, "My Son the Doctor: Aspects of Mobility among American Jews," *American Sociological Review* 34, no. 3 (1969). Slater actually rejects the "scholarship theory," arguing that the Jews' intellectual tradition in the Old World did not readily transfer to the educational and economic demands of the New World.

18. For a thorough discussion of second-generation immigrant Jewish aspirations and experiences, see Deborah Dash Moore, *At Home in America: Second Generation New York Jews* (New York: Columbia University Press, 1981).

19. A summary of this debate is provided in Perlmann, *Ethnic Differences*, 122–62.

20. See Berrol, "Education and Economic Mobility," 261–65.

21. Abram Simon, "The Jewish Child and the American Public School," *Religious Education* 6, no. 6 (1911–1912): 527–28.

22. Michael Olneck, "Americanization and the Education of Immigrants, 1900–1925: An Analysis of Symbolic Action," *American Journal of Education* 97, no. 4 (1989): 401.

23. Kate Rousmaniere, *City Teachers: Teaching and School Reform in Historical Perspective* (New York: Teachers College Press, 1997), 50.

24. Olneck, "Americanization and the Education of Immigrants," 412–13.

25. Isaac B. Berkson, *Theories of Americanization: A Critical Study, with Special Reference to the Jewish Group* (New York: Teachers College, Columbia

University, 1920; reprint, New York: Arno Press and the *New York Times*, 1969), 185.

26. Julius H. Greenstone, "Jewish Education in the United States," in *The American Jewish Year Book 5675*, ed. Herman Bernstein (Philadelphia: The Jewish Publication Society of America, 1914), 127.

27. A summary of these trends can be found in Judah Pilch, ed., *A History of Jewish Education in America* (New York: American Association for Jewish Education, 1969) and Jacob Rader Marcus, *United States Jewry, 1776–1985*, vol. 1 (Detroit: Wayne State University Press, 1989), chaps. 9–10.

28. Mary Antin, *The Promised Land* (New York: Houghton Mifflin, 1912), 168, 103.

29. Berkson, *Theories of Americanization*, 186.

30. See Neil M. Cowan and Ruth Schwartz Cowan, *Our Parents' Lives: Jewish Assimilation in Everyday Life* (New Brunswick, NJ: Rutgers University Press, 1996), chap. 8.

31. Israel Friedlander, "The Problem of Jewish Education in America and the Bureau of Jewish Education of New York City," in *Report of the Commissioner of Education for the Year Ended June 30, 1913*, ed. United States Government (Washington, D.C.: Commissioner of Education, 1913), excerpted in *Jewish Education in the United States: A Documentary History*, ed. Lloyd P. Gartner (New York: Teachers College Press, 1969), 135.

32. Samson Benderly, "Aims and Activities of the Bureau of Education of the Jewish Community (Kehillah) of New York, 1912" (New York: Jewish Community (Kehillah) of New York City, 1912), reprinted in "A Memorial Volume to Dr. Samson Benderly, Leader in American Jewish Education," ed. Alexander M. Dushkin, special issue, *Jewish Education* 20, no. 3 (1949): 106.

33. If the Americanization programs promoted the American civil religion of reverence for the American nation, flag, founding documents (Declaration of Independence, Bill of Rights), government, civil rights, and red-white-and-blue culture, the Judaization programs similarly promoted a type of Jewish civil religion that evolved on the American scene. See Benjamin M. Jacobs, "Affordances and Constraints in Social Studies Curriculum-Making: The Case of 'Jewish Social Studies' in the Early 20th Century," *Theory and Research in Social Education* 37, no. 4 (2009): 515–42. For a discussion of "civil Judaism," see Jonathan Woocher, *Sacred Survival: The Civil Religion of American Jews* (Bloomington: Indiana University Press, 1987).

34. Benjamin M. Jacobs, "Socialization into a Civilization: The Dewey-Kaplan Synthesis in American Jewish Schooling in the Early 20th Century," *Religious Education* 104, no. 2 (2009): 149–65.

35. American Jewry has no chief rabbinate and no definitive *beit din* (religious court).

36. Will Herberg, *Protestant-Catholic-Jew: An Essay in American Religious Sociology* (1955; repr. Chicago: University of Chicago Press, 1983). See our discussion of this work in Chap. 3.

37. For discussions of many of these trends, see the collected works of Jewish educational historians Jonathan Krasner (especially *The Benderly Boys and American Jewish Education*) and Walter Ackerman (especially in Ari Ackerman, Hanan Alexander, Brenda Bacon, and David Golinkin, eds., *"Jewish Education for What?"—And Other Essays*).

38. Eduardo Rauch, *The Education of Jews and the American Community: 1840 to the New Millennium* (Tel Aviv: Tel Aviv University, 2004).

39. Marvin Schick, *A Census of Jewish Day Schools in the United States 2008–2009* (New York and Jerusalem: Avi Chai Foundation, 2009).

40. It is important to distinguish here the modern Jewish day school from the traditionalist Orthodox yeshiva. The majority of day schools in the United States are Orthodox. Many of these schools teach general and Jewish studies, but many others focus almost exclusively on Jewish studies. Our discussion centers on modern Orthodox, Conservative, Reform, and non-denominational community day schools that offer rigorous general studies along with Jewish studies.

41. Cynthia Ozick, *The Cannibal Galaxy* (New York: Alfred A. Knopf, 1983). The novel is based on a story entitled "The Laughter of Akiva," first published in the *New Yorker* magazine on November 10, 1980.

42. *The Cannibal Galaxy*, 26–27.

43. Edmund Fleg (1874–1963) was a French critic and writer whose essay "Why I Am a Jew," published in 1928, is the saga of a person estranged from Judaism who over time comes to embrace it with great feeling.

44. Lee Shulman, "Those Who Understand: Knowledge Growth in Teaching," *Educational Researcher* 15, no. 2 (1986): 4–31; Lee Shulman, "Knowledge and Teaching: Foundations of the New Reform," *Harvard Educational Review* 57, no. 1 (Spring 1987): 1–22.

45. These questions have been examined in great depth in the past half century within the world of Jewish studies on university campuses; however, the worlds of the academy and elementary and secondary Jewish schooling have little interaction. See Robert Chazan and Benjamin M. Jacobs, "Jewish History from the Academy to the Schools: Bridging the Gap," in *Educational Deliberations: Studies in Education Dedicated to Shlomo (Seymour) Fox*, ed. Mordecai Nisan and Oded Schremer (Jerusalem: Keter Publishing House, 2005), 157–80.

46. For a description of the variety of ways that a teacher can present the Bible, see Barry Holtz, "A Map of Orientations to the Teaching of Bible," in *Turn It and Turn It Again: Studies in the Teaching and Learning of Jewish Texts*, ed. Jon Levisohn and Susan P. Fendrick (Brighton, MA: Academic Studies Press, 2013), 26–51.

47. Tali Hyman, "The Liberal Jewish Day School as Laboratory for Dissonance in American Jewish Identity Formation" (PhD dissertation, New York University, 2008).
48. Jack Wertheimer and others, *Generation of Change: How Leaders in Their 20s and 30s Are Reshaping American Jewish Life* (New York: Avi Chai Foundation, 2010).
49. Steven M. Cohen and Laurence A. Kotler-Berkowitz, *The Impact of Childhood Jewish Education on Adults' Jewish Identity: Schooling, Israel Travel, Camping and Youth Groups* (New York: United Jewish Communities, 2004).
50. See, e.g., Jeffrey Kress, *Development, Learning, and Community: Educating for Identity in Pluralistic Jewish High Schools* (Brighton, MA: Academic Studies Press, 2012); Joseph Reimer, *Succeeding at Jewish Education: How One Synagogue Made it Work* (Philadelphia: The Jewish Publication Society, 1997).

BIBLIOGRAPHY

Ackerman, Ari, Hanan Alexander, Brenda Bacon, and David Golinkin, eds. 2008. *"Jewish Education for What?"—And Other Essays by Walter Ackerman.* Jerusalem: Tel Aviv University, University of Haifa, Ben Gurion University.

Antin, Mary. 1912. *The Promised Land.* New York: Houghton Mifflin.

Benderly, Samson. 1949. "Aims and Activities of the Bureau of Education of the Jewish Community (Kehillah) of New York, 1912." New York: Jewish Community (Kehillah) of New York City, 1912. Reprinted in "A Memorial Volume to Dr. Samson Benderly, Leader in American Jewish Education," edited by Alexander M. Dushkin. Special issue, *Jewish Education* 20 (3).

Berkson, Isaac B. 1920. *Theories of Americanization: A Critical Study, with Special Reference to the Jewish Group.* New York: Teachers College, Columbia University. Reprinted, New York: Arno Press and the *New York Times*, 1969.

Berrol, Selma C. 1976. Education and Economic Mobility: The Jewish Experience in New York City, 1880–1920. *American Jewish Historical Quarterly* 65(3): 269.

Bodnar, John. 1985. *The Transplanted: A History of Immigrants in Urban America.* Bloomington: Indiana University Press.

Brumberg, Stephan F. 1986. *Going to America, Going to School: The Jewish Immigrant Public School Encounter in Turn-of-the-Century New York City.* New York: Praeger.

Carlson, Robert A. 1975. *The Quest for Conformity: Americanization through Education.* New York: John Wiley and Sons.

Chazan, Robert, and Benjamin M. Jacobs. 2005. Jewish History from the Academy to the Schools: Bridging the Gap. In *Educational Deliberations: Studies in Education Dedicated to Shlomo (Seymour) Fox*, ed. Mordecai Nisan and Oded Schremer. Jerusalem: Keter Publishing House.

Cohen, Steven M., and Laurence A. Kotler-Berkowitz. 2004. *The Impact of Childhood Jewish Education on Adults' Jewish Identity: Schooling, Israel Travel, Camping and Youth Groups.* New York: United Jewish Communities.

Cowan, Neil M., and Ruth Schwartz Cowan. 1996. *Our Parents' Lives: Jewish Assimilation in Everyday Life.* New Brunswick, NJ: Rutgers University Press.

Cremin, Lawrence A., ed. 1957. *The Republic and the School: Horace Mann on the Education of Free Man.* Classics in Education No. 1. New York: Teachers College Press.

———. 1988. *American Education: The Metropolitan Experience, 1876–1980.* New York: Harper Collins.

Dinnerstein, Leonard. 1982. Education and the Advancement of American Jews. In *American Education and the European Immigrant, 1840–1940*, ed. Bernard J. Weiss, 44–46. Urbana: University of Illinois Press.

Fass, Paula S. 1989. *Outside In: Minorities and the Transformation of American Education.* New York: Oxford University Press.

Friedlander, Israel. 1913. The Problem of Jewish Education in America and the Bureau of Jewish Education of New York City. In *Report of the Commissioner of Education for the Year Ended June 30, 1913*, ed. the United States Government. Washington, DC: Commissioner of Education, 1913. Excerpted. In *Jewish Education in the United States: A Documentary History*, ed. Lloyd P. Gartner. New York: Teachers College Press, 1969.

Gold, Penny Schine. 2004. *Making the Bible Modern: Children's Bibles and Jewish Education in Twentieth-Century America.* Ithaca, NY: Cornell University Press.

Graff, Gil. 2008. *"And You Shall Teach Them Diligently": A Concise History of Jewish Education in the United States, 1776–2000.* New York: Jewish Theological Seminary.

Greenstone, Julius H. 1914. Jewish Education in the United States. In *The American Jewish Year Book 5675*, ed. Herman Bernstein. Philadelphia: The Jewish Publication Society of America.

Herberg, Will. 1955. *Protestant-Catholic-Jew: An Essay in American Religious Sociology.* Chicago: University of Chicago Press. Reprinted, 1983.

Holtz, Barry. 2013. A Map of Orientations to the Teaching of Bible. In *Turn It and Turn It Again: Studies in the Teaching and Learning of Jewish Texts*, ed. Jon Levisohn and Susan P. Fendrick. Brighton, MA: Academic Studies Press.

Hyman, Tali. 2008. The Liberal Jewish Day School as Laboratory for Dissonance in American Jewish Identity Formation. PhD dissertation, New York University.

Jacobs, Benjamin M. 2009a. Affordances and Constraints in Social Studies Curriculum-Making: The Case of 'Jewish Social Studies' in the Early 20th Century. *Theory and Research in Social Education* 37(4): 515–542.

———. 2009b. Socialization into a Civilization: The Dewey-Kaplan Synthesis in American Jewish Schooling in the Early 20th Century. *Religious Education* 104(2): 149–165.

Kaestle, Carl F. 1983. *Pillars of the Republic: Common Schools and American Society, 1780–1860*. New York: Hill and Wang.

Krasner, Jonathan B. 2011. *The Benderly Boys and American Jewish Education*. Waltham, MA: Brandeis University Press.

Kress, Jeffrey. 2012. *Development, Learning, and Community: Educating for Identity in Pluralistic Jewish High Schools*. Brighton, MA: Academic Studies Press.

Marcus, Jacob Rader. 1989. *United States Jewry, 1776–1985*. Vol. 1. Detroit: Wayne State University Press.

Mondale, Sarah, and Sarah B. Patton, eds. 2001. *School: The Story of American Public Education*. Boston: Beacon Press.

Moore, Deborah Dash. 1981. *At Home in America: Second Generation New York Jews*. New York: Columbia University Press.

Olneck, Michael. 1989. Americanization and the Education of Immigrants, 1900–1925: An Analysis of Symbolic Action. *American Journal of Education* 97(4): 398–423.

Ozick, Cynthia. 1980. The Laughter of Akiva. *New Yorker*, November 10.

———. 1983. *The Cannibal Galaxy*. New York: Alfred A. Knopf.

Perlmann, Joel. 1988. *Ethnic Differences: Schooling and Social Structure among the Irish, Italians, Jews, and Blacks in an American City, 1880–1935*. New York: Cambridge University Press.

Pilch, Judah, ed. 1969. *A History of Jewish Education in America*. New York: American Association for Jewish Education.

Rauch, Eduardo. 2004. *The Education of Jews and the American Community: 1840 to the New Millennium*. Tel Aviv: Tel Aviv University.

Reimer, Joseph. 1997. *Succeeding at Jewish Education: How One Synagogue Made it Work*. Philadelphia: The Jewish Publication Society.

Roth, Philip. 1994. The Conversion of the Jews. *Goodbye Columbus*. New York: Vintage.

Rousmaniere, Kate. 1997. *City Teachers: Teaching and School Reform in Historical Perspective*. New York: Teachers College Press.

Schick, Marvin. 2009. *A Census of Jewish Day Schools in the United States 2008–2009*. New York: Avi Chai Foundation.

Schoem, David. 1989. *Ethnic Survival in America: An Ethnography of a Jewish Afternoon School*. Atlanta, GA: Scholars Press.

Shulman, Lee. 1986. Those Who Understand: Knowledge Growth in Teaching. *Educational Researcher* 15(2): 4–31.

———. 1987. Knowledge and Teaching: Foundations of the New Reform. *Harvard Educational Review* 57 (1, Spring): 1–22.

Simon, Abram. 1911–1912. The Jewish Child and the American Public School. *Religious Education* 6(6): 527–528.

Slater, Mariam K. 1969. My Son the Doctor: Aspects of Mobility among American Jews. *American Sociological Review* 34(3): 359–373.

Tyack, David B. 1974. *The One Best System: A History of American Urban Education*. Cambridge, MA: Harvard University Press.

———. 2003. *Seeking Common Ground: Public Schools in a Diverse Society*. Cambridge, MA: Harvard University Press.

Tyack, David B., and Larry Cuban. 1995. *Tinkering Toward Utopia: A Century of Public School Reform*. Cambridge, MA: Harvard University Press.

Ueda, Reed. 1999. Second-Generation Civic America: Education, Citizenship, and the Children of Immigrants. *Journal of Interdisciplinary History* 29(4): 661–682.

Wertheimer, Jack, and Others. 2010. *Generation of Change: How Leaders in Their 20s and 30s Are Reshaping American Jewish Life*. New York: Avi Chai Foundation.

Woocher, Jonathan. 1987. *Sacred Survival: The Civil Religion of American Jews*. Bloomington: Indiana University Press.

Woocher, Jonathan, and Meredith Woocher. 2015. American Jewish Education. In *the American Jewish Year Book 2014*, ed. Arnold Dashefsky and Ira M. Sheskin. New York: Springer.

CHAPTER 5

The Counterculture of American Jewish Education

Education, in the popular imagination, usually involves a place called school and an endeavor called schooling, but in fact the process of education encompasses a much broader complex of experience, learning, and growth. Jerome Bruner, in his seminal exploration of *The Culture of Education* (1996), writes that "it is surely the case that schooling is only one small part of how a culture inducts its young into its canonical ways. Indeed, schooling may even be at odds with a culture's other ways of inducting the young into the requirements of communal living."[1] In that vein, our focus in this chapter is not on schooling, but on all the other ways that the American Jewish community conveys Jewish culture to the rising generation.

If what is conventionally understood as American Jewish education centers on schooling, then virtually everything educational that occurs outside the school context—including in summer camps, community centers, youth groups, museums, heritage tours, social media, adult study sessions, and even the home—not only makes up the rest of the ways that Jewish culture perpetuates itself, but also in a sense constitutes a counterculture. By counterculture, we mean something that pushes up against, or sometimes pushes back against, "the lead-bottomed ballast of the status quo," as Theodore Roszak, the original theorist of the counterculture, put it.[2] Roszak's focus on the rebellious youth that drove the emergence of 1960s counterculture also animates our conception of the term, for, as we shall

© The Author(s) 2017
B. Chazan et al., *Cultures and Contexts of Jewish Education,*
DOI 10.1007/978-3-319-51586-1_5

describe in this chapter, so much of what makes up the Jewish education counterculture is shaped above all by the real or perceived interests, wants, and needs of the rising generation of American Jews. While Jewish schooling, modeled on the civic institution of the public school, essentially represents the traditional concerns of the established Jewish community, the Jewish educational counterculture, responsive to the desires of rank-and-file Jews, attends to the evolving interests of the Jewish people.

Almost from the start, the American Jewish educational enterprise has had a countercultural streak. Jewish summer camps were founded in the first decades of the twentieth century by educational and social progressives who saw the value of taking children out of the hectic routines of the inner cities to provide them with tranquility and recreation in the countryside.[3] Jewish community centers opened in urban (and later suburban) Jewish enclaves, where neither synagogues nor schools could fully capture the attention of increasingly harried and secularized Jewish families, but shared leisure and cultural activities could.[4] Jewish youth groups sought to bring together children with common Jewish backgrounds, interests, and values in contrast to both public schools, which tended toward the homogenization of ethnic groups in an essentially Protestant "American" mold, and Jewish schools, which defined Jewish affiliation in narrow and rigid religious, linguistic, or ancestral modes.

More recently, various alternative *bar/bat mitzvah* experiences, such as Wilderness Torah's B'nature program, seek to vitalize and venerate a traditional Jewish custom while also repudiating the ordinary synagogue- and school-based methods by which children prepare for and participate in this rite of passage. Even BimBam, with its online animated short films about topics in the Hebrew Bible and Jewish tradition, holds the promise of providing a rich Judaics curriculum for Jewish youth without necessitating that they step into a Jewish classroom. In each of these instances, the countercultural turn is not only toward an alternative to the prevailing culture of Jewish schooling, but also away from the parochial context that sustains established Jewish institutions. This pattern of opposition to the so-called Jewish establishment undergirds innovation in Jewish education to this day and has the potential to transform Jewish education and Jewish civilization.[5]

The context for the rise of the contemporary Jewish education counterculture includes changing conceptions of Jewish life in the post-modern, post-ethnic, post-denominational, post-nationalist, "post-everything" world;[6] patterns of increased Jewish demographic diversification and heterogeneity; the democratization of Judaism (i.e., flouting traditional power structures in the Jewish community), including the repudiation of organized Judaism and embrace of individualized Judaism among rank-and-file American Jews; the broader innovation culture—spurred on by dramatic developments in science, technology, communication, transportation, and commerce—that has brought considerable change to the American Jewish landscape; and, substantial communal and philanthropic concern for, and investment in, activities specifically aimed at engaging American Jewish youth in Jewish life. Since the dawn of the twenty-first century especially, the contours of the Jewish education enterprise have changed remarkably. Buzzwords such as "experimentation," "creativity," "new initiatives," "change," and "innovation" dominate discourse in the field, as educators, policymakers, philanthropists, community leaders, parents, and learners alike seek alternative ways to improve upon conventional Jewish educational experiences (i.e., supplementary schools, day schools), or go in entirely novel directions (e.g., social media, gaming). Jewish communities across the United States, and almost every segment of these communities, have devoted efforts and resources toward reform and renewal of Jewish education activities.[7]

This new array of educational efforts and contexts constitutes a Jewish educational counterculture that contrasts with the prevailing American Jewish culture of schooling in several ways, including:

- It is no longer an education system respondent mainly to the organized Jewish communal agenda, but instead consists of various ventures that are more entrepreneurial and grassroots in character.
- It is no longer located exclusively in the brick-and-mortar institutions that once predominated the Jewish communal landscape, but rather takes place in a wide variety of venues that encompass conventional and non-conventional, previously unimagined, and as-yet-to-be imagined means of participating in Jewish education, culture, and life.
- It is more learner-centered and focused on the interests and needs of individual learners, as well as the relevance of the subject matter and skills to the learners, rather than merely perpetuating the Jewish canon and Jewish tradition.
- It is increasingly concerned with the total education of the individual as a social being and with the improvement of society at-large, rather than being limited to the project of instilling Judaism and Jewishness.

- It is more episodic and oriented toward the unique added value of each experience, rather than toward the intensity, regularity, or longevity of the educational program.
- It is more informal and experiential in nature and often less focused on learning particular subject matter and texts.
- It is accessible to an increasingly "mixed multitude" of participants from diverse racial, ethnic, national, socioeconomic, gender, age, ability, sexual orientation, political, denominational, and religious (that is to say, Jewish and/or non-Jewish) backgrounds, identities, and affiliations, and is thereby more inclusive than exclusive.

Above all, whereas Jewish educational initiatives were once developed from the top-down (e.g., formal school programs backed by central boards of Jewish education), they now have been largely supplanted or surpassed by new initiatives growing from the perceived and articulated needs and interests of end-users. Many Jewish education innovators, when looking at interests and goals for educational activities, now begin their planning with the Jewish person in mind, rather than the Jewish community, tradition, or canon.

The potential impact of this countercultural turn on the process of Jewish education cannot be underestimated. Contemporary American Jewish youth are in the main far less inclined than their predecessors to have a strong connection to Jewish texts or to adhere to religious authority—particularly in an organized, institutional, hierarchical form—and are therefore less apt to pursue traditional Jewish study for the sake of enhancing their knowledge of Judaism or their connection to Jewish life.[8] Put another way, today's Jewish youth are not likely to view traditional Jewish study as a religious obligation or even a source of personal fulfillment. Full and unfettered participation in liberal society has given the rising generation a sense of endless possibility with respect to identities and life paths. When choosing their connections and forging their journeys, young Jews seek out various new directions from within the expansive array of alternatives in American society, often with a sense of Jewishness in the background but most often without Judaism lighting the way.[9] Moreover, they describe that sense of Jewishness in terms that emphasize culture and ethnicity more than religion and ritual practice. In light of these shifts among the end-users of Jewish education, providers have had to adjust both the content and delivery mechanisms for Jewish learning, particularly away from the traditional, formal, normative, or ordinary.

THE MAKING OF A JEWISH EDUCATIONAL
COUNTERCULTURE

Progressive Jewish educators in the first decades of the twentieth century had some of the same concerns we still hear about capturing the attention of disaffected American Jewish youth. "Judaism is a problem to those who have to teach it," wrote rabbi/educator Mordecai M. Kaplan in the opening pages of his classic work, *Judaism as a Civilization* (1933): "Parents who wish to inculcate in their children habits and appreciations which are part of Jewish life can no longer do so as a matter of course, but have to argue about it ... with their children... Never did the rising generation so question [Judaism's] value and resent its intrusion into their lives."[10] One of the solutions to this problem, in the view of Kaplan and his contemporaries, was to make part-time Jewish schooling (Sunday schools, afternoon *talmud torahs*) more attractive and enjoyable to students through exciting Jewish-themed projects, arts, and activities, rather than old-style study, memorization, and recitation. Another more adventurous solution was to completely immerse Jewish children in a Jewish environment that was at once entirely artificial—given that it was many miles removed from the pillars of the Jewish home, community, and sanctuary—and also completely authentic—given that it recreated in miniature an idealized Jewish sense of home, community, and sanctuary in its own special place and time: Jewish summer camp. An essential feature of Jewish summer camp was its substantive educational program, including not only instruction in outdoor skills, sports, and recreation, but also—equally or even more importantly—intensive courses aligned with the religious (e.g., prayer skills), political (e.g., Zionism), cultural (e.g., folk dance), and/or linguistic (e.g., Hebrew) missions of the particular camps. Taken together, Jewish summer camp was, in the words of the novelist Chaim Potok, a "two-month sojourn in a recreational-educational Jewish Land of Oz."[11]

What made Jewish summer camps distinct from Jewish schools on one hand (even with their frequent focus on Jewish texts and traditions) and secular summer camps for Jews on the other (where Jewish campers predominantly focused on sports, the arts, and outdoorsy pursuits) was their effort to provide formal Jewish education in an informal milieu. "Informal" did not mean lacking in rigor or seriousness. Rather, it meant learning Jewish living by living Jewishly, rather than studying about it or imitating it in a school setting; the opportunity for immersive, full-time, largely experiential education, rather than synthetic, part-time supplementary education; and the creation of community through shared living, eating, praying, doing, learning, and memory-making, rather than merely through shared lessons in shared classrooms.[12]

Detractors in these early years claimed that Jewish summer camps that convened over a matter of weeks could not possibly be as effective as schools that met over an entire academic year. They also were skeptical about the intensity of the Jewish educational program. How could a discussion of biblical themes under the guidance of a camp counselor outdoors compete with disciplined study of the Torah and its commentaries under the tutelage of a rabbi in a classroom setting? The Jewish content knowledge and skills young people could gain during an hour or two of Jewish programming in between swimming and baseball would not suffice to create lasting Jewish commitments, critics feared. But camp founders believed, and in some ways have proved, that by creating intensive Jewish experiences in a transcendental, spiritual, and tranquil setting, Jewish children would develop a deep appreciation for observing the Sabbath, keeping kosher, speaking Hebrew, and performing religious rites.[13] Indeed, what made Jewish summer camp culturally subversive was the fact that the idealized version of Judaism it presented appeared more authentic and appealing than the Judaism that the campers encountered anywhere else.[14] Furthermore, following a summer (or ideally, summers) of full-time immersion in Jewish life, Jewish living could become so central to the children's day-to-day routines and identification, so pleasurable and important, that they would transfer Jewish observance and sensibilities back to their homes and communities upon their return to everyday life.[15] In this sense, as well, Jewish summer camps were countercultural to the extent that they held out the prospect of succeeding at Jewish education where Jewish schooling apparently had failed: that is, in transforming Jewish households into faithfully Jewish homes.

That said, what has prevented some Jewish summer camps from being countercultural in a more narrow sense is their determination to offer formal instruction in Hebrew and Judaic studies as a central part of the camp program. To cite but one prominent example: Camp Ramah, the Conservative movement-sponsored network of summer camps founded in 1947, dedicated significant resources to the development of its formal education program with renowned consultants from the general education fields of character education and curriculum design, like Joseph Schwab and Ralph Tyler of the University of Chicago. Every aspect of the Ramah experience—every class, daily routine, sports activity, art project, meal, bedtime ritual, prayer service, and so forth—was intentionally planned and implemented with educational objectives and procedures in mind, and toward the end of measurable outcomes. To be sure, there was much for kids to learn just from the experience of living communally with other Jews and observing religious laws. But ultimately Camp Ramah, like many similar Jewish-educationally oriented camps, was fashioned as an intensive formal Jewish education program as well, and an often successful one at that.

The rise of Jewish summer travel experiences in the 1960s offered an alternative to the educational rigidity of Jewish summer camps. USY on Wheels and the USY Israel Pilgrimage would allow teen participants to learn about Jewish life by living Jewishly among Jews round-the-clock and by participating in learning activities including informal discussion at Jewish sites, but without sitting through formal classes. The special benefit of travel as an educational tool is that, inherently, it "enables, even demands, exploration of a subject with all the senses and with the three [learning] modes of cognition, emotion, and behavior."[16] To be sure, the lessons students garner through Jewish travel experiences—which over the years have grown to include pilgrimages to religious sites, heritage tours at historical sites, service learning trips to communities in distress, study abroad programs, and much more—are not simply incidental. On the contrary, educational travel is most valuable when it mixes authentic experiences in situ with intentionally planned lessons, particularly when the aim of the travel is to impart certain ideas and values. However, the predominant curriculum of a travel experience is not what is written in the tour guide's script. Educational travel experiences often operate with the aphorism "seeing is believing" at base. The meaning of the site typically derives foremost from its symbolic power (e.g., the Western Wall), nostalgic pull (e.g., Lower East Side of New York), historical consequence (e.g., Masada), or sheer emotional weight (e.g., Auschwitz), rather than from what guides tell the visitors about the space—hence the term "guide" rather than "teacher."

Another significant component of group travel is the group that travels, for the intensive social environment of the trip contributes to the process of collective memory-building and communal identification in ways that routine cooperative learning in classrooms cannot.[17] Unquestionably the most significant Jewish educational travel program of the early twenty-first century is Taglit-Birthright Israel, a free 10-day heritage trip to Israel for young Jewish adults from communities across the globe. Taglit-Birthright's core mission locates itself in the Jewish journeys of late adolescents and emerging adults. Trips include the opportunity to connect young Jews with other young Jews; young Jews from abroad with young Israelis; young Jews with Israel, its culture, politics, economy, and meaningful places; and ultimately, young Jews with themselves at a crucial point in their intellectual and emotional development, when they are on the precipice of becoming (or not becoming) active citizens of the Jewish community.[18] The key to Taglit-Birthright's success is that it does not make Israel the main subject matter of the trip but rather emphasizes the relationship of emerging young adults with Israel and with other things Jewish, especially Jewish peoplehood. It is the relational aspect of the experience that, more than its other countercultural qualities, sets Taglit-Birthright's educational program apart from the typically instrumental aims of American Jewish schooling. While the trip organizers certainly hope that participants will emerge with an appreciation and love of Israel, they are equally or more eager for young Jewish adults to develop a sense of shared experience, mutual respect, and a yearning for Jewish life.

Those without the time, money, or interest in participating in Jewish heritage tours in the United States or Israel can encounter the historical and contemporary wonders of Jewish civilization in the hundreds of Jewish museums that can be found in cities the world over. On the face of it, museums, as key conduits for cultural transmission, are hardly bastions of counterculture. After all, museums are housed in often magnificent, imposing, or otherwise enthralling edifices that, by their stature and aura alone, help to convey a certain symbolic power, authority, and legitimacy to the museum as a trusted cultural institution. Simply put, museums give off the impression of housing the Truth. Identity museums, such as museums of Jewish heritage, play to this strength by commemorating and celebrating the uniqueness of the focal group and its special contributions to world history and culture.

Jewish museums characteristically present a narrative that vacillates between tragedy (e.g., the Holocaust, anti-Semitism, relics of a destroyed or forgotten past) and triumph (e.g., the State of Israel, Jewish achievements in America, artifacts of a glorified past) in an effort to tug in various ways on their visitors' heartstrings and thereby inspire positive emotional responses. In the process, Jewish museums sometimes massage the message and shade over historical nuance, to be sure, and many provide glitzy edutainment more than genuine edification.[19] However, at a time when surveys of American Jewish sentiments point toward cultural affinities as central to Jewish identification—more so than religion and observance—Jewish museums might be at the vanguard of viable alternatives to traditional Jewish education.[20]

Indeed, while they may be brick-and-mortar, establishment-supported institutions for the perpetuation of heritage, Jewish museums also regularly defy conventional expectations in their efforts to appeal to the interests and tastes of young rank-and-file Jews and non-Jews of diverse backgrounds, in exhibits on avant-garde artists, rock stars, fashion designers, political icono-clasts, and other Jewish cultural and countercultural icons. Critics of Jewish museums decry their lack of Judaic substance and their failure to present Judaism as anything but an irretrievable vestige of the past. But places like the National Museum of American Jewish History (Philadelphia) and Beit Hatfutsot/The Museum of the Jewish People (Tel Aviv) see the value in presenting to contemporary Jews thoughtful and illuminating reflections of the cultural, political, economic, and social worlds they live in today, and how they have been shaped by historical circumstances. In attempting to be a "relevant, cutting-edge museum and cultural center," to "celebrate the multiculturalism of Jewish diversity and adopt an inclusive, pluralis-tic approach," and to "be a force fueling the American spirit of courage and imagination, aspiration and hard work, leadership and service," these museums see themselves as responsive to their contemporary audience's cosmopolitan—that is, not just parochial—proclivities and interests.[21] In so doing, they provide outlets for Jewish cultural expression and learn-ing that are not circumscribed by a formal Judaics curriculum or standard measures of Jewish identification. Part of what makes these Jewish heritage museums countercultural, then, is that they go to lengths to present variet-ies of Jewish life and culture that are anything but conformist. Rather than merely being sites of Jewish cultural transmission, they can also be sites of (as well as provide examples of) cultural transformation.

Jewish community centers (JCCs), which likewise were conceived of as sites of both cultural transmission and transformation when they emerged in the early twentieth century (their dual function famously captured in the wry expression, "shul with a pool"[22]), continue to offer the widest array of cultural, recreational, athletic, Jewish, and general educational activities of any institution in American Jewish life. The primary aim of their educational program is not Jewish literacy per se, but rather the "lifelong process of acquiring Jewish knowledge, skills, attitudes, and val-ues."[23] This kind of socialization process occurs in contexts as varied as monthly lectures on Jewish arts and ideas, weekly Jewish cooking classes, summer Maccabi basketball games, after-school homework tutoring ses-sions, at the café, in the fitness center, and during the Jewish film festival. While they do provide some formal instruction in various subject areas and skills, JCCs are actually superlative settings for informal Jewish educa-tion, insofar as they encourage participants in their programs and activities to learn about partaking in Jewish life through the very act of doing something together with other Jews in a purposefully Jewish setting.

Appropriately enough, JCCs emphasize fostering close relationships between individuals, be they on a peer-to-peer, educator-to-learner, or mentor-to-mentee basis, so that most of the educative process happens interactively rather than didactically. Associating with other Jews in conjoined activity builds civic identity—that is, a sense of Jewish peoplehood, mutual care, and collective responsibility—among members of the JCC community. What is more, because JCCs are open to Jews of all backgrounds and stripes, as well as to non-Jews, they are proving grounds for intergenerational, pluralistic, multicultural community building that is both a reality and desideratum of contemporary American Jewish life.

At one time, secular Jewish families might affiliate with the local JCC as their singular Jewish institution without joining a synagogue or sending their children to Jewish school, as the JCC seemed to provide everything Jewish they might want or need under one roof. But these days, although some JCCs serve as a primary mode of association for elderly Jews, among young adults and young families they no longer hold the place of prominence they once did. Young Men's/Women's Hebrew Associations were founded a century ago when Jews were excluded from YMCAs. Today, exclusion from American social organizations is no longer a key factor in motivating American Jews to associate with one another.

Twenty-first-century JCCs focus on early childhood education, after-school classes, programming for seniors, summer camping, and exercise facilities, and they endeavor to establish themselves as sites of cultural vibrancy and communal relevance. The quest for cultural vibrancy has come partly through the proliferation of JCC-based Jewish film, literary, and music festivals across the United States. The quest for relevance has ranged from upgrading the fitness equipment in order to compete with high-end athletic clubs, to reconfiguring the Jewish educational mission and program to engage children of all ages and from all walks of life in innovative forms of Jewish learning that might provide a fresh, attractive alternative to supplementary Jewish schooling.

The Jewish Journey Project at the JCC Manhattan, for example, "pushes the envelope of what Jewish education can look like," offering many different "pathways into Jewish learning and living," including Hebrew language, spirituality and ritual, social justice and activism, Jewish peoplehood and Israel, and Torah. "Based on your child's passions, curiosities, and preferred mode of learning," the Jewish Journey Project builds "a personalized journey with fun, inclusive, and meaningful courses presented outside of the traditional classroom."[24]

In these JCC ventures, we see the hallmarks of the Jewish education counterculture, particularly the focus on individual interests and experiential learning. At the same time, however innovative they may be, JCCs have found themselves inevitably linked to other old-style, established community institutions—the synagogues, schools, and federations—because of their longstanding function in serving communal needs, or sometimes just by virtue of the fact that they share a campus or building. Fairly or unfairly, their position on the vanguard of American Jewish life is thus challenged.

As these several examples of non-school Jewish education settings suggest the counterculture in American Jewish education evolved piecemeal over the course of the twentieth century and into the twenty-first. While the educational counterculture has tried to compete with Jewish schools in some ways, the culture of American Jewish schooling has remained entrenched. This is partly because summer camps, heritage tours, museums, JCCs, and other informal educational ventures were originally conceived by their sponsors and always have been viewed by their consumers as quintessentially extracurricular activities, rather than as true stand-ins for formal Jewish learning. Whether the potential is there for children to learn as much Jewish history from a 10-day heritage tour or a visit to a museum—or whether a group trip or a site of collective memory can function as an effective agent of socialization rather than instruction— matters little, because of the rooted (if unconscious) perception that true, serious learning happens in schools. These informal non-school educational endeavors are like cousins twice removed to the American Jewish educational system, for they are supplementary to Jewish schooling that is already (mostly) supplementary. The most effective way to legitimate camps and JCCs as Jewish educational institutions has been to offer up a formal Judaics program that could rival what students could get in schools, and so the culture of American Jewish schooling has remained entrenched.

Another reason for the continued dominance of American Jewish schooling is that, historically, educational systems have favored stability rather than change, as education is fundamentally a conservative endeavor designed to preserve and convey cultural norms from one generation to the next.[25] Educational reform policy tends to disintegrate in practice much like a meteor entering the atmosphere: what was once powerful and potentially cataclysmic breaks down mostly to dust, the larger pieces so decimated that they barely make an impact on the surface, let alone the core. What does penetrate the system most often gets retrofitted by administrators and teachers to conform to existing organizational structures.

To provide one example: The Boston-area Kesher afterschool programs for Jewish kids and teens offer an alternative to traditional synagogue-based supplementary schools by teaching Hebrew and Judaics through experiential education and recreation in non-formal settings, through means of drama, Israeli dance, cooking, klezmer, and building with Legos, as well as more traditional areas like Jewish thought, Jewish history, the Jewish calendar, and Hebrew language learning. The idea behind Kesher was, in part, to make supplementary school more like summer camp, given that summer camps have been so successful in their approaches to experiential Jewish education.[26] Here we see, then, the penetration of the counterculture into the reigning culture of Jewish schooling. Nonetheless, even with the fresh, informal, often recreational approach, Kesher (including its middle school programs, which focuses on Jewish texts and Israel/Zionism) still operates with a formal curriculum built on progressively more sophisticated studies of Jewish content leading toward proficiency.[27] "(Not Your Mom's) Hebrew School," declared one observer, touting how much more fun and engaging—and perhaps countercultural—Kesher apparently is.[28] But it's still Hebrew school.

THE "NEXT GEN" OF THE JEWISH EDUCATION COUNTERCULTURE

Changing circumstances in the American Jewish community, beginning in the late twentieth century and accelerating rapidly in the early twenty-first century, have substantially altered the ways in which Jews relate to Jewish life, as well as the ways in which they and their children are (or in some sectors, increasingly are not) educated Jewishly. In the so-called post-everything age, where identity is no longer fixed and unitary but in many ways fluid and textured, Jewish youth see being Jewish as only part of a larger constellation of identities that also encompasses race, ethnicity, gender, socioeconomic status, politics, geography, and sexuality, among other factors.[29] This does not mean that they do not identify as Jews necessarily; to the contrary, the overwhelming majority affirm that being Jewish is an important facet of their identity.[30] But the ways in which they identify Jewishly are complex, conditional, and increasingly individualistic—except perhaps among most traditionalist Jews—and they are no longer neatly aligned with classic denominational, Zionist, or similar associations.

For some, Jewish identification may involve regular observance of Jewish rituals or sporadic attendance at Sabbath and holiday meals; for others, participation in an online Jewish social network or being a consumer of Jewish media, pursuing Jewish studies on a college campus or joining Hillel; for still others, it may be commemorating the Holocaust or going on a trip to Israel, or simply identifying as "just Jewish" without engaging in any overtly Jewish activities. Given the array of entry points to Jewish identification and expression, a sense of collective Jewish identity is diminishing among the rising generation of American Jews.[31] Accordingly, for many young American Jews, long-normative expressions of group membership, such as traditional Jewish educational activities, no longer adequately address the myriad ways they see themselves in the world.[32]

Alongside these changing conceptions of Jewish identity have come significant new patterns of communal diversification and dispersion. About half of American Jews live in cities and most of the rest in suburbs; the largest percentage is in the Northeast, followed by the West, South, and Midwest regions. Significantly, the number of metropolitan areas around the country that have seen rises in Jewish population in the twenty-first century has grown, meaning that American Jews live in more and more diverse areas of the country than they did before. These internal migrations have been facilitated by a variety of social and economic factors, including improvements in technology, communication, and travel that make it easier for job seekers to find work in remote areas and eventually to work remotely. But equally important, the migrations away from long-established areas of Jewish settlement have both been facilitated by and contributed to the erosion of organized American Jewish communal and institutional life. Less emphasis on participation and increased secularization of rank-and-file American Jews in local synagogues, JCCs, schools, and other modes of Jewish association makes it easier for individuals and families to leave rather than cleave to large or traditional Jewish communities. Furthermore, self-identified American Jewish households increasingly have come to include non-Jews (spouses and children) who may or may not be interested in involvement with Jewish communal life.[33] The implication of all these trends for the Jewish educational enterprise is that there are more Jews in far-flung or fledgling Jewish communities who are less likely to have easy access to Jewish schooling or to seek it out. This does not mean that they are totally uninterested in Jewish learning, but they may seek Jewish education in alternative modes and venues.

The voluntary nature of American Jewish organizational life also has evolved over the past generation. American Jews have always been free to choose whether to participate or not participate in the activities of the Jewish community—that is a hallmark of Jewish life in a democracy and free market economy. It was not until recently, however, that the tendency of Jews toward communal affiliation so noticeably reversed course.[34] Indeed, the sociology of Jewishness in America is changing as rank-and-file Jews feel less bound to conventional markers of Jewish affiliation, and the ways that they relate to Jewishness change progressively over the course of their lives.[35] In this age of Judaism à la carte, free will and choice are the rule.[36] Concomitantly, the salience of organized American Jewish life has deteriorated.

There is one more trend of note that is at once countercultural and yet connects back to one of the central elements of conventional Jewish educational culture: namely, the democratization of traditional text study. As manifested in the world of Jewish education, we find increased interest among selected young Jewish adults, even from nontraditional backgrounds, in doing traditional biblical and rabbinic text study as a means of participating in traditional learning in the community but on one's own terms, gaining more personal access to the process of Jewish meaning-making (e.g., Yeshivat Hadar in New York, Pardes Institute in Jerusalem, MakomDC in Washington, Valley Beit Midrash in Phoenix, Svara: A Traditionally Radical Yeshiva in Chicago, and Project Zug nationwide). From the perspective of these (mostly) young adults, Jewish expertise and interpretation are no longer the exclusive province of traditionalist old men, but are also within the ken of aspiring learners of all backgrounds.

The increasingly democratic access to, and participation in, Jewish learning is also represented by the growth of grassroots Jewish educational initiatives. One of the fastest growing Jewish education ventures of the twenty-first century is Limmud, which was started in the UK in the 1980s and spread to North America in the 2000s. Limmud conferences, held from one to several days at a time, gather diverse Jewish learners together for a minds-on, hands-on experience of intensive learning of Jewish texts, rituals, arts and culture, historical issues, and current affairs. According to Limmud's mission, "everyone should be a student and anyone can be a teacher," "learning embraces personal development, knowledge and skills," "volunteerism is a key feature of almost everything we do," "we value accessibility and aim to be accessible to all," and "we value choice in form, content and style in our programs."[37] If ultimately Limmud aims to foster a "community of learning," it does so by encouraging individual choice and self-direction, and by relying on grassroots initiative and volunteer leadership. As one participant put it, "Limmud is a smorgasbord of choose-your-own adventure goodness!"[38] The success of Limmud comes largely from its ability to give learners personal ownership of their Jewish learning experiences, in a meaningful and pleasurable communal context.

The ongoing democratization of Jewish life reflects the extent to which American Jews have adopted and adapted the mores of the surrounding society over time, and continue to do so in the context of increasing fluid relationships to and understandings of identity. In fact, American Jewry in the twenty-first century is among the most thoroughly assimilated Jewish communities in history. We do not use the term "assimilated" here to signify a precipitous decline in Jewish life, but rather to suggest that, with the exception of extreme outliers (e.g., ultra-Orthodox cloistered communities), Jews are by now totally mainstreamed into the general political, social, economic, and cultural fabric of American life. This does not mean that Jews have lost any distinctiveness as an ethno-religious subgroup, but it does mean that Jewish distinctiveness is for the most part unremarkable, appearing alongside many other distinctive, if not exclusive, identities.

America reflexively accommodates the participation of Jews and the influence of Jewish culture in all sectors of society: government, business, popular culture, media, higher education, social clubs, organizations, and so forth. Likewise, American Jews, while overwhelmingly proud of being Jewish, are also predominantly secular and tend to prioritize their secular pursuits, like careers, social networks, and leisure activities, over all things Jewish.[39] Young Jews, especially, are constantly in pursuit of new opportunities, new relationships, new gadgets, new adventures, and new experiences, and judge all of these by whether they are hip, popular, lucrative, and leverage-able, rather than what contributes to Jewish identity and commitment.[40] The writer Irving Howe observed regarding supplementary Jewish schooling in the early twentieth century: "The pupils resent[ed] the *heder* as a theft of time that might be better used playing stickball."[41] While the twenty-first century distractions from Jewish involvement for children, teens, and young adults are quite different, the predicament remains the same.

In this context, many Jewish education reformers have recognized that they have little choice but to become countercultural in order to stay relevant. Within the system of American Jewish schooling, the counterculture takes the form of new, more diverse subject matter (e.g., the introduction of Arabic to the world languages program of some day schools), more dynamic pedagogical methods (e.g., the multiplying of interactive computer-based applications, such as gaming, for learning Judaic subjects), more experientially oriented educators (e.g., the proliferation of day school administrative positions such as "school life coordinator," "director of trips and special programs," and "service learning supervisor," and supplementary school directors of "youth and family programming"), more out-of-the box structures (e.g., the emergence of Jewish Montessori schools and Hebrew language public charter schools throughout the United States), more secular achievements in Jewish settings (e.g., massive investments in STEM education, arts, and sports in day schools), more imaginative ways of preparing children for *bar/bat mitzvah* (e.g., the Reform movement's B'nai Mitzvah Revolution), and even more elastic aims (e.g., changing approaches to Israel education focusing on diverse narratives, relationships, and experiences, rather than simply *ahavat Yisrael* or "Love of Israel"). Some of these are bold changes to be sure, and others are more like question marks or exclamation points within the grammar of Jewish schooling. It is yet to be seen whether these ventures will bring about a paradigm shift in standard Jewish educational practices.

Nevertheless, the twenty-first century has seen a spectacular explosion of exciting Jewish educational initiatives spring up out of the creative minds and bold visions of innovative educators and communal leaders who no longer accept the proposition that Jewish learning necessarily happens in schools, classrooms, and other formal settings. Hundreds of transformative Jewish start-up organizations have been created since 2000 with the express purpose of providing innovation in Jewish organizational life, and particularly, the Jewish education enterprise. The range of these activities is incredibly vast, encompassing all sorts of new ways for engaging students with Jewish-related content (culture, texts, values, rituals), and it impinges on a host of traditional and nontraditional venues for educational activity, including websites, arts spaces, media, historical sites, cultural centers, and the outdoors. Several of these start-up initiatives are undergirded by new theories and research being generated by an expanding and talented cadre of Jewish education scholars, and they are being supported by a small but highly motivated pool of venture philanthropists eager to discover the "next big thing" in Jewish education—especially a viable alternative to supplementary Jewish schooling.[42] Indeed, we are in the midst of the most creative age in the modern American Jewish education enterprise since its founding in the early twentieth century.[43]

Take, for instance, the massive proliferation of electronic Jewish media outlets online, including digitized newspapers, magazines and webzines, intellectual journals, blogs, social networks, audio and video streaming sites, web commerce, and institutional and organizational websites, in addition to Jewish learning sites that emphasize Judaic content, rituals, history, Hebrew language, the Jewish calendar, lifecycle events, archival materials, web-based instruction and gaming, and a plethora of other topics and modalities. Jewish home schooling, an alternative to institutional Jewish schooling that is gaining in popularity, can be accomplished with the internet as the main guide.[44] But, in fact, anyone seeking knowledge about Judaism, Jewish culture, Jewish life, and Jewish identification, can do so with only a few clicks or taps from just about anywhere in the globe. There is no need for a school, formal curriculum, or teacher for this kind of learning.

To be sure, not all the material generated by online Jewish content providers is high-quality, discerning, or accurate, nor is much of it designed to facilitate the progressive development of Jewish literacy or commitment. Nonetheless, the sheer access and exposure of today's Jews (and others interested in Judaism) to a boundless array of Jewish information, peer networks, media, culture, texts, and all other things Judaic and Jewish, facilitates experiential Jewish learning, Jewish identification, and even Jewish community-building of a kind and extent that previously could only be imagined.

One other type of outside-the-classroom Jewish learning that has seen steady growth in recent years is service learning. Capitalizing on millennials' stated interests in working toward social betterment in the wider world, various Jewish social justice, civic action, community organizing, and disaster relief organizations have emerged or have added programs, with the express aims of involving American Jewish young adults and children in effective service to others through active, direct participation in social issues projects within distressed communities and with people in need, in a meaningful Jewish context with a Jewish learning component. These programs, which can last from a day or a week to several months or a year, address wide-ranging systemic issues such as international development, poverty, sustainability, refugee and immigrant settlement, food justice, social welfare, education, elder care, disability services, discrimination, civil rights, and emergency relief work. Physical labor, directly meeting human needs, building infrastructure, teaching, outreach, mentoring, and consulting are among the various activities participants engage in during service learning programs. A related area that has seen explosive growth in recent years is Jewish outdoor, food, and environmental education. Here, the aim is to help repair the natural world and the human relationship to it through education in and practices of sustainable agriculture, preservation and conservation, ecological responsibility, recycling and resource reduction, nutrition and health, animal rights, and other environmental issues.

While most Jewish service learning and environmental education programs are universalistic in their mission and reach, they explicitly address Jewish content and contexts and teach participants to see their work through the lens of Jewish values. The majority of young adult participants in these programs report that they have grown as caring individuals and active community members and have acquired invaluable leadership skills. They also report increased involvement in Jewish communal activities following their service learning experiences, thus demonstrating the programs' utility as vehicles for socialization into the American Jewish community.[45]

* * *

Taken together, most of the twenty-first-century Jewish education initiatives we have discussed here have in common the criteria for the Jewish educational counterculture we laid out at the beginning of this chapter: they are grassroots, experiential, episodic but intensive, accessible, portable, and responsive to the interests and needs of learners. Above all, they represent faith in the prospect that Jewish education happens practically everywhere.[46] Indeed, ironically enough, today's inventive Jewish education programs, while ostensibly fresh, innovative, and countercultural, may actually signal a return to the more holistic Jewish educational framework of old, in which Jewish education happened not merely in schools, but rather in the normal course of everyday life activities at home and in the community. In this framework, Jewish education happens not only intentionally via formal curricula and programs, but also incidentally via the experiences individuals have in relation to social institutions and to each other.[47] At summer camps, in JCCs, on heritage tours, in museums, in distressed communities, on the farm, in synagogues, at libraries; in youth groups, workplaces, social justice organizations; on athletic fields, in public spaces, on television, on satellite radio, in cyberspace; and in families, homes, and around the *Shabbat* dinner table—friends, peers, relatives, adults, children, mentors, guides, educators, co-workers, fellow Jews, and fellow citizens are educating each other and themselves all the time. Of course, for these incidental educational experiences to be Jewishly meaningful, they need to be intentionally oriented—however overtly or subtly—toward Jewish values, rituals, texts, identity, or whatever else is apt given the participants, mission, and context.

But meaningful, serious, countercultural Jewish education—often outside of formal, even parochial, settings—need not be viewed by American Jewish youth as a theft of time that could be better used doing something else. The goals of these activities, and the accomplishments of the most successful ones, are to make them part of the essence of the learners' being; to enhance Jews' enthusiasm for learning Jewish content and consuming Jewish culture with friends; to go beyond pre-packaged lessons on *tikkun olam* and inculcate the ability and disposition to make service work a regular part of their civic and Jewish responsibility; to develop their appetite for festive Jewish meals and Jewish rituals more extensively; and in all ways, to have young Jews not simply take part in a constructed Jewish educational enterprise or artificial Jewish community, but to partake of and participate organically in Jewish civilization.

NOTES

1. Jerome Bruner, *The Culture of Education* (Cambridge, MA: Harvard University Press, 1996), x.
2. Theodore Roszak, *The Making of a Counter Culture* (Garden City, NY: Anchor Books, 1969), 3.
3. Miriam Heller Stern, *"Your Children—Will They Be Yours?" Educational Strategies for Jewish Survival, the Central Jewish Institute, 1916–1944* (doctoral dissertation, Stanford University, 2007).
4. David Kaufman, *Shul with a Pool: The "Synagogue-Center" in American Jewish History* (Hanover, NH: University Press of New England, 1999).
5. Jonathan Woocher, "Reinventing Jewish Education for the 21st Century," *Journal of Jewish Education* 78, no. 3 (2012): 182–226.
6. Benjamin M. Jacobs, "Problems and Prospects of Jewish Education for Intelligent Citizenship in a Post-everything World," *Diaspora, Indigenous, and Minority Education* 7, no. 1 (2013): 39–53.
7. Jonathan Woocher and Meredith Woocher, "Jewish Education in a New Century: An Ecosystem in Transition," in *American Jewish Year Book 2013*, ed. Arnold Dashefsky and Ira Sheskin (New York: Springer, 2014), 3–57.
8. David Bryfman, *Generation Now: Understanding and Engaging Jewish Teens Today* (New York: The Jewish Education Project, 2016).
9. UJA-Federation of New York, *Insights and Strategies for Engaging Jewish Millennials* (New York: UJA-Federation of New York, 2016). See also Bethamie Horowitz, *Connections and Journeys: Assessing Critical Opportunities for Enhancing Jewish Identity* (New York: UJA-Federation of Jewish Philanthropies of New York, 2000).

10. Mordecai M. Kaplan, *Judaism as a Civilization: Toward a Reconstruction of American-Jewish Life* (New York: Macmillan, 1933), ix.

11. Chaim Potok, "Introduction," in *A Worthy Use of Summer*, ed. Jenna Weissman Joselit and Karen S. Mittelman (Philadelphia: National Museum of American Jewish History, 1993), 7.

12. Barry Chazan, *The Philosophy of Informal Jewish Education*, http://www.infed.org/informaljewisheducation/informal_jewish_education.htm

13. Amy L. Sales and Leonard Saxe, *"How Goodly Are Thy Tents": Summer Camps as Jewish Socializing Experiences* (Hanover, NH: University Press of New England, 2004).

14. Janet Aviad, "Subculture or Counterculture: Camp Ramah," *Studies in Jewish Education* 3 (1988): 197–225. Aviad claims that the camp could not be countercultural in the end because the intensification of Jewish life among kids, potentially against the wishes of the parents, would alienate the camp's supporters.

15. Stern, *"Your Children—Will They Be Yours?"*.

16. Eric H. Cohen, "Travel as a Jewish Educational Tool," in *International Handbook of Jewish Education: Part One*, ed. Helena Miller, Lisa Grant, and Alex Pomson (London: Springer, 2011), 616.

17. Shaul Kelner, *Tours That Bind: Diaspora, Pilgrimage, and Israeli Birthright Tourism* (New York: NYU Press, 2012); Barbara Kirshenblatt-Gimblett, *Destination Culture: Tourism, Museums, and Heritage* (Berkeley: University of California Press, 1998).

18. See the Taglit-Birthright Israel website: http://taglitww.birthrightisrael.com/TaglitBirthrightIsraelStory/Pages/default.aspx

19. For a strong critique of Jewish identity museums, see Edward Rothstein, "The Problem with Jewish Museums," *Mosaic*, February 1, 2016, http://mosaic-magazine.com/essay/2016/02/the-problem-with-jewish-museums/.

20. Pew Research Center, *A Portrait of Jewish Americans: Findings from a Pew Research Center Survey of US Jews* (Washington, DC: Pew Research Center, 2013).

21. The Museum of the Jewish People, "About Beit Hatfutsot," http://www.bh.org.il/about-us/about-beit-hatfutsot/; National Museum of American Jewish History, "Mission Statement," http://www.nmajh.org/MissionStatement/.

22. Kaufman, *Shul with a Pool*.

23. Barry Chazan, *What Is Jewish Education in the JCC?* (New York: Jewish Community Centers Association, 1996), 10.

24. http://www.jccmanhattan.org/attach/JJP_Brochure.pdf

25. Larry Cuban, "Curriculum Stability and Change," in *Handbook of Research on Curriculum*, ed. Philip W. Jackson (New York: Macmillan, 1992), 216–47.

26. Sales and Saxe, *"How Goodly Are Thy Tents."*

27. See, e.g., http://www.keshernewton.org/overview.html.
28. Elicia Brown, "(Not Your Mom's) Hebrew School," *JW Magazine*, Fall 2011, http://www.jwmag.org/page.aspx?pid=2999.
29. Anna Greenberg, *Grande Soy Vanilla Latte with Cinnamon, No Foam: Jewish Identity and Community in a Time of Unlimited Choices* (New York: Reboot, 2006).
30. UJA-Federation of New York, *Insights and Strategies for Engaging Jewish Millennials.*
31. Pew Research Center, *A Portrait of Jewish Americans.*
32. Bryfman, *Generation Now.*
33. See, e.g., Matthew Boxer, Janet Krasner Aronson, Matthew A. Brown, and Leonard Saxe, *Greater Seattle Jewish Community Study 2014* (Seattle: Jewish Federation of Greater Seattle, 2014).
34. Pew Research Center, *A Portrait of Jewish Americans.*
35. Bethamie Horowitz, "The Importance of a Navigational Perspective in the Study of Contemporary American Jews: Response to the Sklare Lecture," *Contemporary Jewry* 35, no. 2 (2015): 137–45.
36. Debra Nussbaum Cohen, "Shul's Out Forever? Millennials Customize and Curate Faith to Create Their Own Judaism," *The Forward*, February 2, 2016, http://www.forward.com/news/333451/shuls-out-forever-millennials-customize-and-curate-faith-to-create-their-ow/
37. http://www.limmudinternational.org/images/stories/Articles/livalues.pdf
38. Steven M. Cohen and Ezra Kopelowitz, *The Limmud International Study. Jewish Learning Communities on a Global Scale* (Jerusalem: Research Success Technologies, 2011).
39. Pew Research Center, *A Portrait of Jewish Americans.*
40. UJA-Federation of New York. *Insights and Strategies for Engaging Jewish Millennials.*
41. Irving Howe, *World of Our Fathers: The Journey of the East European Jews to America and the Life They Found and Made* (New York: Harcourt Brace Jovanovich, 1976; reprinted, New York: Schocken Books, 1989), 201.
42. Woocher and Woocher, "Jewish Education in a New Century."
43. One of the major signposts of this transformation was the renaming of the Board of Jewish Education of Greater New York, which was founded by Samson Benderly in 1910 as the Bureau of Jewish Education of New York City, as The Jewish Education Project in 2010 on the occasion of the organization's centennial. The Jewish Education Project has been one of the central incubators for innovation ever since.
44. Avigayil Perry, "Home Schooling: A Growing Trend," *Jewish Action*, Fall 2015, www.ou.org/jewish_action/08/2015/home-schooling-a-growing-trend/.
45. Ilana Aisen and Anya Manning, *Building a Field: 2010–11 Year End Report on Immersive Jewish Service-Learning Programs* (New York: Repair the

World, 2011); Jewish Outdoor Food, Farming, & Environmental Education, *Seeds of Opportunity: A National Study of Immersive Jewish Outdoor, Food, and Environmental Education (JOFEE)* (New York: Hazon, 2014).

46. Ari Y. Kelman, "Education Everywhere," *eJewishPhilanthropy*, December 18, 2012, http://ejewishphilanthropy.com/education-everywhere/

47. John Dewey, *Democracy and Education: An Introduction to the Philosophy of Education* (New York: Macmillan, 1916); Lawrence A. Cremin, "Public Education and the Education of the Public," *Teachers College Record 77*, no. 1 (1975): 1–12.

BIBLIOGRAPHY

Aisen, Ilana, and Anya Manning. 2011. *Building a Field: 2010–11 Year End Report on Immersive Jewish Service-Learning Programs.* New York: Repair the World.

Aviad, Janet. 1988. Subculture or Counterculture: Camp Ramah. *Studies in Jewish Education* 3: 197–225.

Boxer, Matthew, Janet Krasner Aronson, Matthew A. Brown, and Leonard Saxe. 2014. *Greater Seattle Jewish Community Study 2014.* Seattle: Jewish Federation of Greater Seattle.

Brown, Elicia. 2011. (Not Your Mom's) Hebrew School. *JW Magazine*, Fall. http://www.jwmag.org/page.aspx?pid=2999.

Bruner, Jerome. 1996. *The Culture of Education.* Cambridge, MA: Harvard University Press.

Bryfman, David. 2016. *Generation Now: Understanding and Engaging Jewish Teens Today.* New York: The Jewish Education Project.

Chazan, Barry. 1996. *What Is Jewish Education in the JCC?* New York: Jewish Community Centers Association.

———. 2002. *The Philosophy of Informal Jewish Education.* http://www.infed.org/informaljewisheducation/informal_jewish_education.htm

Cohen, Debra Nussbaum. 2016. Shul's Out Forever? Millennials Customize and Curate Faith to Create Their Own Judaism. *The Forward*, February 2. http://www.forward.com/news/333451/shuls-out-forever-millennials-customize-and-curate-faith-to-create-their-ow/.

Cohen, Eric H. 2011. Travel as a Jewish Educational Tool. In *International Handbook of Jewish Education: Part One*, ed. Helena Miller, Lisa Grant, and Alex Pomson. London: Springer.

Cremin, Lawrence A. 1975. Public Education and the Education of the Public. *Teachers College Record* 77(1): 1–12.

Cuban, Larry. 1992. Curriculum Stability and Change. In *Handbook of Research on Curriculum*, ed. Philip W. Jackson, 216–247. New York: Macmillan.

Dewey, John. 1916. *Democracy and Education: An Introduction to the Philosophy of Education.* New York: Macmillan.

Greenberg, Anna. 2006. *Grande Soy Vanilla Latte with Cinnamon, No Foam: Jewish Identity and Community in a Time of Unlimited Choices.* New York: Reboot.

Horowitz, Bethamie. 2000. *Connections and Journeys: Assessing Critical Opportunities for Enhancing Jewish Identity.* New York: UJA-Federation of Jewish Philanthropies of New York.

———. 2015. The Importance of a Navigational Perspective in the Study of Contemporary American Jews: Response to the Sklare Lecture. *Contemporary Jewry* 35(2): 137–145.

Howe, Irving. 1976. *World of Our Fathers: The Journey of the East European Jews to America and the Life They Found and Made.* New York: Harcourt Brace Jovanovich. Reprinted, New York: Schocken Books, 1989.

Jacobs, Benjamin M. 2013. Problems and Prospects of Jewish Education for Intelligent Citizenship in a Post-everything World. *Diaspora, Indigenous, and Minority Education* 7(1): 39–53.

Jewish Outdoor Food, Farming, & Environmental Education. 2014. *Seeds of Opportunity: A National Study of Immersive Jewish Outdoor, Food, and Environmental Education (JOFEE).* New York: Hazon.

Kaplan, Mordecai M. 1933. *Judaism as a Civilization: Toward a Reconstruction of American-Jewish Life.* New York: Macmillan.

Kaufman, David. 1999. *Shul with a Pool: The "Synagogue-Center" in American Jewish History.* Hanover, NH: University Press of New England.

Kelman, Ari Y. 2012. Education Everywhere. *eJewish Philanthropy*, December 18. http://ejewishphilanthropy.com/education-everywhere/.

Kelner, Shaul. 2012. *Tours That Bind: Diaspora, Pilgrimage, and Israeli Birthright Tourism.* New York: NYU Press.

Kirshenblatt-Gimblett, Barbara. 1998. *Destination Culture: Tourism, Museums, and Heritage.* Berkeley: University of California Press.

Perry, Avigayil. 2015. Home Schooling: A Growing Trend. *Jewish Action*, Fall. www.ou.org/jewish_action/08/2015/home-schooling-a-growing-trend/.

Pew Research Center. 2013. *A Portrait of Jewish Americans: Findings from a Pew Research Center Survey of US Jews.* Washington, DC: Pew Research Center.

Potok, Chaim. 1993. Introduction. In *A Worthy Use of Summer*, ed. Jenna Weissman Joselit and Karen S. Mittelman. Philadelphia: National Museum of American Jewish History.

Roszak, Theodore. 1969. *The Making of a Counter Culture.* Garden City, NY: Anchor Books.

Rothstein, Edward. 2016. The Problem with Jewish Museums. *Mosaic*, February 1. http://mosaicmagazine.com/essay/2016/02/the-problem-with-jewish-museums/.

Sales, Amy L., and Leonard Saxe. 2004. *"How Goodly Are Thy Tents": Summer Camps as Jewish Socializing Experiences*. Hanover, NH: University Press of New England.

Stern, Miriam Heller. 2007. "Your Children—Will They Be Yours?" Educational Strategies for Jewish Survival, the Central Jewish Institute, 1916–1944. Dissertation, Stanford University.

UJA-Federation of New York. 2016. *Insights and Strategies for Engaging Jewish Millennials*. New York: UJA-Federation of New York.

Woocher, Jonathan. 2012. Reinventing Jewish Education for the 21st Century. *Journal of Jewish Education* 78(3): 182–226.

Woocher, Jonathan, and Meredith Woocher. 2014. Jewish Education in a New Century: An Ecosystem in Transition. In *American Jewish Year Book 2013*, ed. Arnold Dashefsky and Ira Sheskin, 3–57. New York: Springer.

Epilogue

We have traversed centuries, venues, and worldviews in this book to examine diverse contexts and cultures of Jewish education, in order to understand fully the challenges and opportunities of American Jewish education. Our journey began with an ancient Israelite educational culture that focused on living lives rooted in a vision of the holy, the human, the historical, the good, the moral, and the divine. Subsequent Jewish educational cultures explicated and built on this original narrative to meet the needs of the diverse Jewish and general cultures in which Jews lived. The saga of Jewish education over time is a story of persistence, as we saw in the pre-modern context; adaptation, as we saw in the modern context; and innovation, as we see in the contemporary American context. In this epilogue, we suggest guidelines for a twenty-first-century American Jewish educational culture shaped by legacies of the past, dynamics of the present, and dreams of the future.

In Search of a *Paideia*

The first task of twenty-first-century American Jewish education is to answer the as yet unanswered and fundamental question of twentieth-century Jewish life: Jewish education for what? To be sure, much was accomplished by the architects of twentieth-century American Jewish education. Schools were built, camps and youth movements were created, courses of study were developed, textbooks were published, teachers

© The Author(s) 2017
B. Chazan et al., *Cultures and Contexts of Jewish Education,*
DOI 10.1007/978-3-319-51586-1

and informal educators were hired, children were enrolled, websites were created, Hebrew was spoken, heritage tours were guided, museums were visited, social networks were formed, and summer *Shabbat* services were held by the lake. Young American Jews dutifully learned various family, synagogue, and lifecycle customs and rituals, and they also regularly heard about the importance of Jewish community, heritage, and survival.

At the same time, twentieth-century American Jewish education was without a clear overarching vision or mission. American Jewish educators and their students rarely dealt with—and more importantly seldom answered—the most basic questions about the Jewish worldview: Who am I? How do we know? What is the good? How does history happen? Why do bad things happen? How can we change ourselves? What values are important? What is Judaism? Who are the Jewish people? Why does being Jewish matter? Twentieth-century Jewish education was not rooted in addressing these core questions nor in proposing a vision of personal ideals and virtues regarded as essential. It mainly was rooted, instead, in knowing about Jewish things, learning how to do Jewish things, and developing emotional ties to Jewish things.

The American Jewish educational enterprise has lacked what we have called in this book a *paideia*—that is, a theory and practice of education that asks and proposes answers to questions about how we should live our lives, what the role of reason is in life, how history is shaped, and what our core virtues and values are. From the early years to one's final days, such questions are central to the human experience, and the preoccupation with them has implications for key components of education—including aims, contents, pedagogies, and pedagogues—as well as, more broadly speaking, the way we envision our place in the cosmos. These questions are at the heart of character or values education, which is fundamentally what Jewish education is or should be about. Jewish education, like most forms of humanistic education, is part of the enterprise of learning to be human. In this sense, at its core Jewish education cannot simply be about Jewish literacy, heritage, advocacy, or survivalism, but must be about the moral, intellectual, spiritual, and cultural development of our youth and ourselves.

Jewish civilization over the ages has put forth a plethora of existential questions that cry out for answers. God in Eden asks Adam, "Where are you?" Cain, after killing his brother Abel, asks, "Am I my brother's keeper?" Abraham at Sodom asks God, "Will not the judge of all the earth do justice?" The Psalmist asks God, "What is man that you are mindful of him?" The ancient rabbi Hillel asks, "If I am not for myself, who will be for me?

But if I am only for myself, who am I?" Medieval rabbi and philosopher Moses ben Maimon (Maimonides) asks in his *Guide to the Perplexed*, "Did the universe have a beginning? Will it ever end?" and "What is the nature of evil?" The Hasidic master Levi Yitzchak of Berditchev, in his famous prelude to the Kaddish prayer, asks God, "What do you want of your people Israel? What have you demanded of your people Israel?" Modern Hebrew poet Rachel, sitting on the shores of the Sea of Galilee, asks, "Was it real or did I only dream a dream?" Twentieth-century theologian Rabbi Abraham Joshua Heschel asks, perhaps most fundamentally, "Who is Man?"

Jewish tradition over the ages has been preoccupied with critical questions as much as correct answers. Some of the traditional answers to the great questions continue to be engaging and compelling to Jews today; other answers that may have been meaningful in former days have been reexamined and readdressed in modern times. The engagement with a tradition that asks questions about life's core issues and proposes answers worthy of serious consideration is what contemporary Jewish education should be about.

Twentieth-century American Jewish life and education were understandably focused on the agenda of integration into a new society, while at the same time attempting to retain some link with its past. Moreover, the overwhelming issues of twentieth-century Jewish life—mass migration to the United States in the early part of the century, the destruction of six million European Jews in the 1930s and 1940s, and the struggle for and realization of the State of Israel in 1948—surely affected the agenda of American Jewish education. The preoccupation with integration into America and the circumstances and events of twentieth-century Jewish life, along with the need for the school to largely replace the home as educator of Jewish rites and mores, shaped the contexts and cultures of American Jewish education. Lost along the way were the important theological, epistemological, moral, and existential issues related to being a Jew—and being a human—in the world, issues that could have imbued the enterprise with meaning, relevance, and significance. American Jewish education has had an agenda, to be sure, but it has lacked a *paideia*. The result is that American Jewish education often has seemed adrift or off course, like a hollow vessel bobbing at sea.

Twenty-first-century American Jews are a different lot in a different place. They are no longer an immigrant people struggling to find their way in a new world—they are by now fully integrated and active shapers of American life and culture. Their agenda is not that of their parents, grandparents, and great-grandparents. Millennials are preoccupied with meaning-making rather than absorbing inherited meaning; with multiple identities rather than with an exclusively or primarily Jewish identity; and with creating communities of consent rather than descent. They are a generation that asks the kinds of core questions we have discussed above. And they appear open and even predisposed to a Jewish education that deals with critical issues about Jewish life and the human condition. In short, twenty-first-century young American Jews are in many ways a people in search of a *paideia*.

FROM *PAIDEIA* TO PRACTICE

A *paideia* is more than a theoretical vision; it is, in fact, the key to all aspects of a larger educational practice. A *paideia*-based education does not define curriculum as a list of courses, but rather as a comprehensive blueprint and strategic plan of topics, texts, methodologies, and practices for realizing educational ideals. The idea of curriculum encompasses the "overt" (what is actually taught); the "covert" (non-scripted learnings that occur in the context of educating); and the "null" (ideas very consciously omitted and not taught).[1] Twenty-first-century Jewish education requires a radical reconceptualization of curriculum, which shifts the focus from the teaching of disconnected subject matters such as Bible, Hebrew, customs, and ceremonies to a holistic perspective of Jewish civilization as a culture that over the ages has dealt with the key issues of human life. Such a curriculum frames the Jewish educational effort as the interaction with the Jewish experience through a variety of prisms—history, sociology, core texts, ritual, language, land, spirituality, and values—that together comprise the multi-dimensional rubric of Jewish civilization.

The overt curriculum of this approach is the story of a people birthed in a specific place, nurtured on core values, and existing for thousands of years in multiple venues and contexts. This story is spelled out through core texts that convey key ideas and underlying values; historical study that traces the highways and byways of Jewish life over time and place; and religious rituals, foods, songs, and poetry that convey the arts and culture of the people. The covert curriculum—school atmosphere, decor, artifacts, and human relations—reflects and exemplifies the ideas, values, and practices of Jewish civilization. This civilization should be cast as a vibrant, value-rooted, human culture that has learned to adapt to many diverse settings (both hostile and receptive), not framed by the lachrymose tendency to present Jewish life as a saga of ongoing suffering, persecution, and eventual redemption. The null curriculum—which heretofore has consisted of the works and ideas of general culture that were regarded as beyond the purview of Jewish education—should itself be nullified and should now be accessed for the purpose of examining Jewish civilization from outside it as well as from within.

PEDAGOGY

Educationists such as John Dewey, Jerome Bruner, and Lee Shulman have taught us that good pedagogies, or methodologies of teaching and learning, are closely linked to the subjects and disciplines being taught and studied.[2] Biblical texts, for example, by their very nature invite critical thinking, discussion, and deliberation over and beyond their literal meaning, for they are replete with parables and precepts. Thus, the rabbinic methodology of study, interpretation, and commentary encourages even young students to become contemporary commentators. Similarly, disciplinary methods of inquiry can be equally applied to the study of a Jewish topic as they would be applied to the study of a general topic, as with the study of Jewish history and sociology or Hebrew language and literature. Ultimately, the central methodologies of educating for values in Jewish education are the general tools of values education, which include inquiry, analysis, understanding, reflection, discussion, interaction, engagement, and modeling. The pedagogy of Jewish values education is a person-centered, value-driven, inquiry-oriented dialogic approach, which enables students to engage with great ideas and big questions.

EDUCATORS

Who are the educators needed to populate our twenty-first-century Jewish educational institutions and teach our children and youth? Our discussion of *paideia*, curriculum, and pedagogy makes it abundantly clear that twenty-first-century American Jewish education requires a reconsideration of who teaches, how they teach, and what type of preparation they need. The new Jewish educator—the pre-school teacher, the day school teacher, the supplementary school teacher, the rabbi, the camp counselor, the Israel tour leader, the Jewish communal professional, and the youth group advisor—is someone who admires Jewish civilization, loves teaching, and respects learners. He or she believes in the possibility of opening minds, hearts, and hands. His or her priority is not to impose values but rather to enable students to see, to think, to reflect, to choose, and to do. As envisioned by educationist Parker Palmer, good teaching comes from the identity and integrity of the teacher and from the courage to help students weave a life for themselves.[3] The Jewish educators we need should be role models, guides, and facilitators. They must have core literacy in Jewish texts, history, and ideas, along with personal and pedagogical skills to make these values and events come alive and resonate with contemporary learners. Indeed, while the subject matter of the Jewish educator's work is Jewish civilization, the true subject of the educator's enterprise is, foremost, the learner. As the educational philosopher Nel Noddings reminds us, educators must not merely care *about* passing on knowledge and perpetuating culture; they must also care *for* the inquisitive minds, impressionable hearts, and precious souls in their charge. It is an awesome task deserving of reverence.[4]

Unfortunately, the neglected child of American Jewish professional life has long been the front-line Jewish educator—precisely the person who has the most personal contact with young Jews. Given that parents entrust teachers with the Jewish education of their children, it is incumbent upon parents to treat educators with a proper measure of respect and appreciation. This is not simply about increasing teacher salaries and benefits, though those areas must be addressed as well. Rather, there is a communal responsibility to create a new vision of education as an exciting, respectable, and honored profession with rigorous standards, specializations, required knowledge, skill sets, and competencies, as well as a well-defined ladder of professional advancement. New criteria for content literacy, pedagogic skills, linguistic proficiency, supervised fieldwork, mentoring, and credentialing must be established in the professional preparation of Jewish educators, so as to enable the emergence of a new cadre of educators who have the knowledge, experience, and competencies to prepare Jewish youth for active and effective membership in the Jewish community and the world at large.

Such a new vision for and version of the Jewish educator might well attract a group of talented young people inspired by the opportunity to teach, which could lead to a revolution in both the popular image of who is a Jewish educator and the reality of who is educating and what they are teaching. The metamorphosis of Jewish education needs to begin with the educator, whose work in turn needs to begin with the learner.

A Culture of Education

In Chapter 3, we saw how contemporary American Jewish life is a significant educator in its own right. As means of socialization, the books, films, television programs, magazines, sites, organizations, workplaces, community centers, and public lives of American Jews are sometimes as important, or even more important, than the subject matter learning that schools provide. Indeed, the "campus" of American Jewish education is not limited to the Jewish day or supplementary school nor to what children learn during their *bar/bat mitzvah* preparations. The words of Deuteronomy 6:4–9—the centermost prayer in Jewish liturgy, the *Sh'ma*—succinctly describe the arenas of education as sitting at home, walking on the way, lying down, and rising up. Given the limitless dynamics of modern communication, travel, and connectedness, the campus of contemporary Jewish education encompasses synagogue, youth groups, cyberspace, the groves of academe, museums, historical Jewish sites, the State of Israel, and many other venues. Jewish education must shift from its Americanized model of education as schooling, to a vision of an expansive "campus of Jewish education" encompassing new technologies and platforms, new institutional and non-institutional settings, new pedagogies, and new kinds of learners. The task is to reshape the current school-based model with a twenty-first-century 24/7/365 "campus" of multiple portals into Jewish experience. Rather than necessarily distancing young Jews from Jewish experiences, the new world of the global village opens limitless opportunities for experiencing Jewish civilization in all its diversities.

Authority

Perhaps the most difficult issue on the agenda of twenty-first-century American Jewish education is the question of who controls the agenda. In biblical and rabbinic times, the notion of authority was clear: "At Sinai Moses received the Torah and handed it over to Joshua who handed it to the prophets who in turn gave it to the men of the Great Assembly."[5] This chain of authority was passed on to the authors of the Mishnah and the Talmud and to centuries of rabbis, religious authorities, and learned and respected teachers. For the segment of Jewry that has resisted modernity, the chain of transmission still places authority in the hands of a group of learned rabbinic leaders. But for the majority of contemporary Jews, the acceptance of modernity created a radical shift in longstanding Jewish understandings of authority, with reason, history, and human engagement assuming new centrality. For American Jewish education, the shift of authority has proven to be dramatic.

While many are respected figures, most contemporary rabbis would be the first to acknowledge that they are not definitive Jewish educational authorities. School headmasters are dedicated professionals whose duties encompass recruitment, organization, fundraising, and staff supervision, but these positions increasingly do not enable them to become definitive authorities on Jewish education. There have been only a few significant Jewish educational figures in the twentieth and twenty-first century with the stature or the power to serve as true authorities in the formulation and implementation of policy in Jewish education. The various central national agencies of Jewish education have been suggestive rather than legislative. Moreover, since Jewish schooling is mostly local in venue and governance, there is a sense in which every school, its rabbi and/or its education director, and its school board are together their own local authority. Indeed, the American Jewish model of shared power between professionals and lay people has created a culture in which education is frequently the bailiwick of the professional-lay partnership. This model has certain advantages, but—as twentieth-century American public educational leaders came to understand—many issues are inherently or especially professional in nature, and thus a balance of local input and autonomy and regional and national professionalism is essential.

It is unlikely that contemporary Jewish education could (and not desirable that it should) revert to the authoritative models of yesteryear, but it is not viable for Jewish education to be without some twenty-first-century modes of authority, and not prudent to continue ahead without creating some new viable alternatives. The Jewish educational world would do well to consider new frameworks that substantively involve academic scholars, Jewish curriculum specialists, foundation professionals, and reflective practitioners coalescing into some form of academy or institute of Jewish education that could serve as a valuable source of authority and influence.

CAN IT HAPPEN?

In this book, we have examined a long path of Jewish civilization that has been populated by people, ideas, cultures, and practices that have taken the notion of education very seriously and have marshaled human and financial capital and an ongoing commitment to perpetuate the venture.

The agenda that we have proposed for twenty-first-century American Jewish life is weighty and calls for a significant coordinated communal effort among leadership, stakeholders, professionals, and consumers in the educational enterprise, along with ideas, frameworks, materials, and abundant resources to respond to the challenge. We suggest a comprehensive reconceptualization of the American Jewish education enterprise. Is this really feasible?

We believe that contemporary Jewish life provides us with enough examples to support the claim that change can happen and that a renewed *paideia* and praxis can be shaped to create an engaging and powerful world of Jewish education. The emergence of academic Jewish studies has created a reservoir of content-rich writings and people who are potentially important forces in seriously upgrading the curriculum writ large. A thoughtful group of Jewish educational academics has emerged as well, who can contribute to shaping *paideia*, pedagogy, and pedagogues. There is a cadre of remarkable headmasters, teachers, and schools across North America that are exemplars of what might be; rather than being seen as exceptions to the rule, they might come to be regarded as models to emulate. Creative new countercultural initiatives dealing with *bar/bat mitzvah* training, teaching Hebrew, Jewish travel, adult learning, and experiential education are spawning new networks and frameworks for Jewish learning. There is a new culture of innovation, change, and creativity that is carving out innovative routes and settings for Jewish education. Surely one of the most significant developments in recent years is the emergence of a new generation of philanthropists committed to enriching the field. They have made programs, training, and resources available for start-up organizations, professional development, and both conventional and outside-the-box ventures aimed at the improvement of Jewish education. The possibility of coordinating efforts between philanthropies and Jewish educational and communal leaders might offer new vistas for a system, vision, and practice of twenty-first-century American Jewish education.

The twenty-first-century agenda that we have framed differs from agendas and processes that currently characterize contemporary Jewish education, insofar as we propose the possibility of a route much longer and with results less immediately tangible than the "impact study" or "next big thing" approaches might yield. Admittedly, the longer path sometimes seems too time-consuming when the needs are apparently so immediate. However, there are times when the seemingly longer path proves to be ultimately the more proactive and fruitful route. The new *paideia* of Jewish education will not be built in a day. But if it is crafted carefully over the course of a generation, it can have lasting reverberations for generations to come. This is our belief and our hope for twenty-first-century Jewish education.

Coda

This book opened with the following proposition: The human quest for knowledge takes many forms. Sometimes individuals and groups attempt to understand aspects of their immediate surroundings for the joy of knowing for its own sake, and sometimes they seek knowledge for utilitarian purposes. Perhaps the most significant pursuit of knowledge involves the profound quest to understand oneself and one's universe and to translate that understanding into constructive and meaningful living.

The cultures of Jewish education throughout the ages have been impressive, thoughtful, and powerful forces in responding to this human quest to understand oneself and the universe, so as to translate that understanding into meaningful living. Jewish tradition, history, and culture address the most essential questions about life and offer well-conceived and varied answers worthy of consideration. It is our hope that the Jewish youth of today and tomorrow will be afforded the possibility of accessing this eternal wellspring of questions and answers that matter.

Notes

1. Eliot W. Eisner, *The Educational Imagination: On Design and Evaluation of School Programs*, 3rd ed. (New York: Macmillan, 1994).
2. John Dewey, *Democracy and Education: An Introduction to the Philosophy of Education* (New York: Macmillan, 1916); Jerome Bruner, *The Process of Education* (Cambridge, MA: Harvard University Press, 1960); Lee Shulman, "Those Who Understand: Knowledge Growth in Teaching," *Educational Researcher* 15, no. 2 (1986): 4–31.
3. Parker Palmer, *The Courage to Teach: Exploring the Inner Landscape of a Teacher's Life* (San Francisco: Jossey-Bass, 2007).
4. Nel Noddings, *The Challenge to Care in Schools: An Alternative Approach to Education* (New York: Teachers College Press, 1992).
5. *Pirkei Avot* 1:1.

BIBLIOGRAPHY

Bruner, Jerome. 1960. *The Process of Education*. Cambridge, MA: Harvard University Press.

Dewey, John. 1916. *Democracy and Education: An Introduction to the Philosophy of Education*. New York: Macmillan.

Eisner, Eliot W. 1994. *The Educational Imagination: On Design and Evaluation of School Programs*. 3rd ed. New York: Macmillan.

Noddings, Nel. 1992. *The Challenge to Care in Schools: An Alternative Approach to Education*. New York: Teachers College Press.

Palmer, Parker. 2007. *The Courage to Teach: Exploring the Inner Landscape of a Teacher's Life*. San Francisco: Jossey-Bass.

Shulman, Lee. 1986. Those Who Understand: Knowledge Growth in Teaching. *Educational Researcher* 15(2): 4–31.

INDEX

A

Abraham, 3, 142
Adam and Eve, 2, 142
Alexander the Great, 12, 18
Allen, Woody, 76
America. *See* United States
American Association for Jewish
    Education (AAJE), 96–7
American Dream, 67, 86, 89
American Israel Public Affairs
    Committee (AIPAC), 75
American Jewish Committee, 69, 79
American Jewish Congress, 79
American Jewish contemporary
    authors, 76
American Jewish life
    American Jews and Israel, 73–6
    being Jewish in America, 80–1
    communal cohesion, 78–80
    expansive Jewish opportunities, 65–9
    foundations of, 60–4
    Holocaust and, 71–3
    lessons from immigrant
        experience, 64–5
    organizing, 70–1

secular American Jewish culture, 76–7
American Jewish schooling, 83–5
    culture and counterculture, 106–7
    culture of, 92–100
    culture of schooling, generally, 85–6
    day schools, 101–6
    public schooling, 87–92 (*see also*
        (counterculture of American
        Jewish education))
American Jews, prominent
    artists, 67
    composers, 77
    contemporary writers, 76–7
    feminist leaders, 69
    gangsters, 68
    novelists and dramatists, 76
    politicians and business leaders, 67
    popular musicians, 77
    popular theologians, 69, 71
Anti-Defamation League, 79
Antin, Mary, 64
anti-Semitism, 62, 105, 124
As a Driven Leaf (Steinberg), 69
Assyrian Empire, 8–9, 12, 13, 19
authority, 147–8. *See also* rabbis

© The Author(s) 2017
B. Chazan et al., *Cultures and Contexts of Jewish Education*,
DOI 10.1007/978-3-319-51586-1

B

Babylonian Empire, 9–10, 12, 13, 19
Babylonian Talmud, 15
bar/bat mitzvah, 96, 98, 99, 118,
    132, 147, 149
Beit Hatfutsot/The Museum of the
    Jewish People (Tel Aviv), 125
Benderly, Samson, 95, 97
Ben-Gurion, David, 74
Berlin, Irving, 67, 77
Berrol, Selma, 90
Beth Shalom Congregation
    (Philadelphia), 70
Bible. *See* Hebrew Bible; New
    Testament; Torah
Biltmore Program, 73
BimBam, 118
Brandeis, Louis D., 67, 73
Bruner, Jerome, xx, 117, 145
Bundist (socialist) schools, 83
Bureau of Jewish Education (New
    York City), 95, 97

C

Cahan, Abraham, 64
Call It Sleep (Roth), 64
Camp Ramah, 122–3
Canaan, 2, 5, 7–8, 10, 19, 28
Cannibal Galaxy, The (Ozick), 103
Catholicism, 24, 34, 39, 42, 44, 88,
    91, 102, 103
Central Synagogue (New York
    City), 100
Chorin, Aaron, 50
Christianity, 13, 19–20. *See also*
    Catholicism; Protestantism
    and American Jewish life, 61–3, 71, 72
    conversion to, 27
    Jewish transition to Western
        Christendom, 23–8
    missionizing campaigns, 27–8
    and modernity, 32–3, 35, 37, 39,
        44–52
    and public schooling, 91

Commentary (magazine), 69
complementary schools, 96. *See also*
    supplementary Jewish schools
Conservative Judaism, 69, 71, 78, 96,
    98, 122
conversion, religious, 21, 27
counterculture of American Jewish
    education, 117–20, 134–5
    foundations of, 121–8
    Jewish community centers (JCCs),
        125–7, 129, 134
    Jewish museums, 124–5
    next generation of, 128–35
    summer camps, 117–18, 121–3,
        127–8, 134
    summer travel experiences and
        heritage tours, 123–4
Cremin, Lawrence, xxi, 85
Cuban, Larry, 86
Culture of Education, The (Bruner),
    xx, 117
curriculum, xxi, 86, 87, 96–101
    counterculture Jewish education,
        118, 122–3, 125, 128, 133
    day schools, 102–6
    dual curriculum, 42, 103–6
    paideia and, 144–5, 148, 149
    standards, 73

D

David, Larry, 76
day school associations, 97
day schools, 83, 84, 101–7, 132, 145
Denial (film), 73
Der Forverts (The Forward,
    newspaper), 64
Destruction of the European Jews, The
    (Hilberg), 72
Dewey, John, 145
Diary of Anne Frank, The, 72
diaspora, 10, 13, 19, 27
Dinnerstein, Leonard, 89
Dreyfus Affair, 43
Dylan, Bob, 77

E

education. *See* American Jewish schooling; counterculture of American Jewish education; day schools; pre-modern Jewish education; supplementary Jewish schools
definition of, 85
educational leadership, 10–14, 18, 148
educators, preparation of, 145–6
Eichmann in Jerusalem (Arendt), 72
emancipation, Jewish, 43, 60, 62, 63, 66, 70, 71
endogamy, 98, 107
England, xviii, 25, 39, 52
English language, 64, 75, 87, 92
Enlightenment, 18, 20, 32, 42, 47, 55–6, 60–1, 63, 88, 106
Eternal Light, The (radio and television program), 71
excommunication, 21
exile, xvii, 5–7, 9–10, 12–14
Exodus (Uris), 74
exodus from Egypt, 4, 16, 46

F

family foundations and philanthropies, 97
feminist leaders, 69
Five Books of Moses, 98, 105. *See also* Torah
France, xviii, 31, 36–9, 43, 60, 61
Frank, Anne, 72
French Revolution, xv, 36
Friedlander, Israel, 94

G

Germany, xviii, 39, 44, 52, 61, 72, 88
Ghetto, The (Wirth), 64
globalization, xix
God, existence of, xvii, 19
God in Search of Man (Heschel), 71

Gold, Penny Schine, 89
Goodbye Columbus (Roth), 67
Gospels, 47–9, 62
Great Britain, 61, 73
Guide for the Perplexed, A (Horn), 69

H

Hadassah Magazine, 74
Hanukkah, 99
Hebrew Bible, 1–2, 7, 8, 10, 14, 27, 45–8, 50, 118
Leviticus, 2
Deuteronomy, 4, 7–8, 147
II Kings, 8–9 (*see also* (Torah))
Hebrew language, xviii, 42, 74, 96, 98–100, 105, 106, 121–2, 126, 128, 132, 133, 142, 145, 149
Hebrew schools, 70, 84–5, 95–6, 99–100, 128. *See also* supplementary Jewish schools
Hebrew Union College-Jewish Institute of Religion, 69, 97
heders (one-room schoolhouses), 83, 84, 89, 95, 104, 131
Herberg, Will, 98
Heschel, Abraham Joshua, 71, 143
higher education, 68, 102, 131
high holidays, 99
Hirsch, Samson Raphael, 51
Holocaust, xiv, 71–4, 105, 129
Holocaust, The (television mini-series), 72
Holocaust denial, 73
Hungry Hearts (Yezierska), 64

I

identity
Jewish, xvi, xviii–xix, 40, 44, 48, 54–6, 63–4, 96, 98, 106, 126, 129, 131, 144
national, 72, 73, 88, 91
religious, xvi, 40–4, 55, 61, 63

immigration, xiv, xviii, 25
and American Jewish life, 61–3,
71–4, 78, 83, 87–8
lessons from immigrant
experience, 64–5
and public schooling, 87–92, 95
Islam, xiv, xv, 19, 20, 23, 24, 26–7,
32, 33, 39
Israel
American Jews and, 73–6
Biblical Israel, xviii, 2–13, 16–17,
22, 27
Land of Israel, xviii, 10–13, 19, 39,
41, 73
State of Israel, 74–5, 98, 124, 143,
147
Zionism, 41–2, 68, 73–5, 95,
121, 128
Israeli writers, 75
Ivrit b'Ivrit (a method of learning
Hebrew by speaking Hebrew), 96

J
Jazz Singer, The (film), 65
Jefferson, Thomas, 49–50
Jerusalem, 10, 13, 39, 77, 103, 130
Temple of, 10, 11, 16, 22
Jesus of Nazareth, 25–6, 33, 47,
49–50, 52, 62
*Jewish Catalog: A Do-It-Yourself Kit,
The*, 69
Jewish community centers (JCCs),
125–7, 129, 134
Jewish education consultancies, 97
Jewish Education Service of North
America (JESNA), 97
Jewish National Fund, 74
Jewish studies, 68–9, 88, 104–6, 127,
129, 149
Jewish Theological Seminary of
America, 69, 71, 94, 97
J Street, 75

Judah *ha-Nasi*, 15
Judaism as a Civilization (Kaplan), 121
Judgement at Nuremberg (Kramer), 72

K
Kaplan, Mordecai M., 69, 121
Kesher afterschool programs
(Massachusetts), 128
Koufax, Sandy, 68

L
Lag Ba'Omer, 99
Lebanon War, 75
Limmud, 130
Lipstadt, Deborah, 73
Locke, John, 34–5, 51

M
Maimonides, Moses (Rambam), 54, 143
Man is Not Alone (Heschel), 71
meaning-making, 77, 130, 144
Meet the Fockers (film), 77
Meir, Golda, 77
Melting Pot, The (Zangwill), 64
Mesopotamia, 8, 10–13, 16, 23
Millennial generation, 128–33, 143–4
miracles, Biblical, 45–7, 50
Mishnah, 7, 15, 147
missionizing campaigns, 25–7
modernity, xiii–xiv, xvii, xix–xx, xxi,
19–20, 28, 31–2
and challenges to traditional
religion, 45–8
and educational perspectives, 55–6
and egalitarian society, 35–9
and historic achievements of Jewish
people, 52–5
and Jewish educational facilities, 44
and Jewish religious worldview, 48–51
and organizational patterns, 42–4

and reconceptualizing
Jewishness, 39–42
and role of religion, 33–5
and separation of church and state,
xvi, xviii, 35
and societal organizations, xvi–xvii
monotheism, 19, 25, 28, 31–3, 45. *See
also* Christianity; Islam
Moses, 2, 10, 12, 14–17, 22, 46, 147
Mosaic message, 4–7
museums, 124–5

N
Napoleon Bonaparte, 38
nationalism, 41–2, 63, 73, 78, 118.
See also Zionism
National Jewish Monthly, 74
National Museum of American Jewish
History (Philadelphia), 125
Nazism, 72, 74, 103
New Testament, xxi, 45–7. *See also*
Gospels
Night (Wiesel), 72
Noddings, Nel, 146

O
Oral Torah, 15, 17–18, 22, 27
Orthodox Judaism, 69, 78, 101,
104–6, 131
Ozick, Cynthia, 103–4

P
paideia, xiv, xxi, 86, 141–4
and authority, 147–8
and culture of education, 147
and educators, 145–6
and pedagogy, 145
and practice, 144–5
Palestine, 12–15, 46, 73–5
Palestinian Talmud, 15
Passover, 26, 99

Peace Now, 75
Peace of Mind (Liebman), 71
peace treaties, 75
pedagogy, 145
Persian Empire, 10, 12, 19
pre-modern Jewish education, 1–2
authority and stability, 18–23
Biblical Israel, 2–4
and Jewish worldview, 28
Mosaic message, 4–7
and the prophets, 7–14
and rabbis, 10–14
transition to Western
Christendom, 23–8
private schools, 101, 102, 105, 106.
See also day schools
Promised Land, The (Antin), 64
Prophets, 7–12, 14–17, 22, 46, 50,
98, 147
Protestant-Catholic-Jew (Herberg),
70, 98
Protestant Reformation, 18, 35, 61
Protestantism, 34, 35, 39, 42, 44, 87,
88, 91, 95, 98, 118
publishing houses, 69, 97
Purim, 99

Q
quotas in higher education, 68, 88

R
rabbinical schools, 69
rabbis, xvi, 147
and American Jewish life, 69, 70, 78
and American Jewish schooling, 85,
94, 97–8, 104
educational efforts and achievements
of, 14–17
and educational leadership, 10–14
and Mishnah, 7, 15, 147
and pre-modern Jewish education,
7–8, 10–17, 22

Rachel the Poetess, 143
racism, 72, 73, 75. *See also*
    anti-Semitism
Rashi's Daughters (Anton), 69
Red Tent, The (Diamant), 69
Reform Judaism, 50, 69, 71, 78, 96,
    98, 100, 132
Rise of David Levinsky, The (Cahan), 64
Rise of the Goldbergs, The (radio
    program), 65
Roszak, Theodore, 117
Roth, Philip, 67, 76
Rousmaniere, Kate, 91

S
Sabbath, 16–17, 103, 129
Schindler's List (film), 72
Schoem, David, 85
schools and schooling. *See* American
    Jewish schooling; counterculture
    of American Jewish education;
    day schools; pre-modern Jewish
    education; supplementary Jewish
    schools
  definition of, 85–6
Schwab, Joseph, 122
self-governance, 19–20, 32, 37, 60
self-segregation, 49
seminaries, 69, 71, 78, 86, 94, 97
separation of church and state, xvi, 9,
    35–6, 55, 60, 79
sermons, 17, 27
Shavuot, celebration of, 99
Shoah (Lanzmann), 72
Shulman, Lee, 145
Simon, Abram, 90
Six-Day War, 75
Sodom and Gomorrah, 3, 142
Spielberg, Steven, 67–8, 72
Streisand, Barbra, 77
summer camps, 107, 117, 118, 121–3,
    127–8, 134
summer travel experiences, 123

Sunday schools, 84, 92, 95, 107, 121.
    See also supplementary Jewish
    schools
supplementary Jewish schools, 84–6,
    93–100, 102, 106–7, 119, 121–2,
    127, 128, 131–2, 147
  Hebrew schools, 70, 84–5, 95–6,
    99–100, 128
  Sunday schools, 84, 92, 95, 107, 121
Survival in Auschwitz (Levi), 72
synagogues
  and American Jewish life, 65,
    69–71, 73, 74, 76, 78–9, 85
  and American Jewish schooling, 85,
    92, 93, 96, 99–100, 103
  and counterculture of American
    Jewish education, 118, 126–9,
    134, 142
  and curriculum, xxi
  and modernity, 40, 43, 55
  and pre-modern Jewish education,
    16–17, 28
synagogue schools, 96. *See also*
    supplementary Jewish schools

T
Taglit-Birthright Israel, 76, 123–4
Talmud, 15, 147
talmud torahs (community-sponsored
    schools), 83, 95, 121
Tanakh, 1–2
teachers' colleges, 97, 100
Temples, 10, 11, 16, 22
Thomas of Monmouth, 26
Torah, 4, 7, 11–12, 17–18, 22,
    98, 147
  Oral Torah, 15, 17–18, 22, 27
  study of, 51, 94, 122, 126
Tu B'Shevat, 99
Tyack, David, 86
Tyler, Ralph, 122
tzedakah (philanthropy and social
    justice), 96

U

Union of American Hebrew
    Congregations (later Union of
    Reform Judaism), 96
United Nations, 74
United States, xviii, 31, 49, 56. *See also*
    American Jewish life; American
    Jewish schooling; counterculture
    of American Jewish education
United Synagogue of America (later
    United Synagogue of
    Conservative Judaism), 96
USY Israel Pilgrimage, 123
USY on Wheels, 123

W

War Against the Jews, The
    (Dawidowicz), 72
What Makes Sammy Run?
    (Schulberg), 67
*When Bad Things Happen to Good
    People* (Kushner), 71
Wiesel, Elie, 72, 73

Wilderness Torah, 118
Wilderness wandering, 2, 4, 6, 10, 16,
    23, 27, 46
World War II, xix, 67, 70, 72, 74, 105.
    See also Holocaust
Wright, Frank Lloyd, 70

Y

Yentl (film), 77
Yerushalmi, Yosef Hayim, 54–5
Yeshiva University, 69, 97
yeshivas (all-day schools), 83, 89, 95,
    101. *See also* day schools
Yiddish, 64, 103
Yitzchak, Levi, of Berditchev, 142–3
Yom Kippur War, 75

Z

Zakhor (Yerushalmi), 54–5
Zionism, 41–2, 68, 73–5, 95,
    121, 128
Zola, Emile, 43